All the best,

Kev

Canberra, 26 April 2002

Ireneusz Iredyński

Selected one-act plays for radio

Routledge Harwood Polish and East European Theatre Archive
A series of books edited by Daniel Gerould, Graduate School, City University of New York, USA

Volume 1
To Steal a March on God
Hanna Krall
Translated and with an introduction by Jadwiga Kosicka

Volume 2
Alternative Theatre in Poland
1954–1989
Kathleen Cioffi

Volume 3
Country House
Stanisław Ignacy Witkiewicz
Translated and with an introduction by Daniel Gerould

Volume 4
The Trap
Tadeusz Różewicz
Translated by Adam Czerniawski

Volume 5
Polish Romantic Drama
Harold B. Segal

Volume 6
The Mannequins' Ball
Bruno Jasienski
Translated and with an introduction by Daniel Gerould

Volume 7
Leading Creators in Twentieth-Century Czech Theatre
Jarka Burian

Volume 8
Encounters with Tadeusz Kantor
Krzysztof Miklaszewski
Edited and translated by George Hyde

Volume 9
Ireneusz Iredyński: Selected one-act plays for radio
Edited by Kevin Windle

Please see the back of this book for other titles in the Routledge Harwood Polish and East European Theatre Archive series

Ireneusz Iredyński

Selected one-act plays for radio

Edited by Kevin Windle

London and New York

First published 2002
by Routledge
11 New Fetter Lane, London EC4P 4EE

Simultaneously published in the
USA and Canada by Routledge
29 West 35th Street, New York, NY 10001

Routledge is an imprint of the Taylor & Francis Group

Typeset by EXPO Holdings
Printed and bound in Great Britain by
MPG Books Ltd, Bodmin

British Library Cataloguing in Publication Data
A catalogue record for this book is available from the British Library

Library of Congress Cataloging in Publication Data
Iredyński, Ireneusz, 1939–
[Plays. English. Selections]
Selected one-act plays for radio/Ireneusz Iredyński; edited by Kevin Windle.
p. cm. – (Routledge Harwood Polish and East European Theatre Archive; 9)
Translated by Wojciech Dabrowski and Kevin Windle.
Includes bibliographical references.
Contents: Ibis – Before the lecture – The radio – Nobody dances like that now – The terrarium – First prize – The window – The kidnapping – The garden gate.
1. Iredyński, Ireneusz, 1939– Translations into English. 2. Radio plays, Polish – Translations into English. I. Windle, Kevin, 1947 – II. Dabrowski, Wojciech. III. Title. IV. Series.

PG7168.R4 A24 2002
891.8′5273–dc21

2001048576

ISBN 0–415–27503–2

Contents

Introduction to the Series

The *Routledge Harwood Polish and East European Theatre Archive* makes available in English translation major works of of Poland's dramatic literature as well as monographs and critical studies on Polish and East European playwrights, theatre artists and stage history. Although emphasis is placed on the contemporary period, the archive also encompasses the ninteenth-century roots of modern theatre practice in Romanticism and Symbolism. The individual plays will contain authoritative introductions that place the works in their historical and theatrical contexts.

Daniel Gerould

Introduction

In Poland's rich and varied theatrical tradition Ireneusz Iredyński stands as something of an *enfant terrible*. He was born into a tumultuous age and was no doubt largely shaped as a writer and dramatist by the times in which he lived, times which were marked by trauma and brutality unusual even in the troubled history of Poland. Being born in 1939, his earliest childhood was spent in a period of war and foreign occupation, followed immediately by the hardships of the post-war period and the country's forced transition to Soviet-style socialism – for many only slightly less traumatic than the occupation.

He made his début in literature with a poem at the age of sixteen and at twenty already had a volume of poetry to his credit. Before long he had published short stories and novels and was noted as a Polish 'angry (and very gifted) young man'.[1] He moved on to demonstrate even greater versatility with stage plays, film-scripts and plays for radio. In the later years of his short life he maintained a steady output of full-length plays for the theatre, being described as 'virtually dramatist in residence' at Warsaw's Teatr Polski not long before his alcoholic self-destruction in late 1985 at the age of forty-six.[2]

Iredyński has been credited with writing a kind of 'autobiography of his generation' in his novels and plays.[3] Each generation in the twentieth-century history of Poland has been moulded by specific national events. This, no doubt, is also the case in many other countries, but in Poland a series of key events is ever present in the national consciousness and recorded in a kind of transparent code by the names of the months in which they took place. To take only a few modern examples, we have 'September' (in which the Wehrmacht overran the country in 1939); 'October' (the high point of destalinization in 1956, when the country seemed poised to overthrow its communist rulers or face Soviet intervention); 'December' (the Baltic Seaboard strikes and rebellion of

1970, brutally put down by government forces); the 'Polish August' (1980, when the Gdansk accords were forced upon a reeling government by the rising power of organized labour); and again 'December' (when that government under General Jaruzelski reasserted control by imposing martial law on 13th December 1981).

The late Andrzej Drawicz (1932–1997) wrote in his autobiography of the events which marked his own generation, contrasting his age-group with those only a few years older, who experienced combat, and those mostly younger than himself who formed the core of youthful resistance to the regime in the late 'sixties.[4] Iredyński falls between the generations of Drawicz and the students of the late 'sixties. Born in 1939, he was not of an age to retain any memory of life in pre-communist peace-time. More significantly, his schooling roughly coincided with the years of uncompromising Stalinist rule, the late 'forties and early 'fifties, when under the new authorities, closely controlled from Moscow, Poland's very identity came close to being subsumed into that of its all-powerful neighbour and isolation from Western influences was rigorously policed.

This period finally came to an end in the crisis of 1956, three years after Stalin's death, when Iredyński was in his late teens. There followed a public reappraisal of the Stalinist years and some (as yet still limited) contact with the culture of the West. When the crisis of 'October' passed, the country found itself under what promised to be a more liberal communist regime headed by Władysław Gomułka and for a time some relatively open public discussion could take place. Rebellious writers and film-makers found a public forum. The stories of Marek Hłasko, the poems of Adam Ważyk and the films of Andrzej Wajda formed part of the cultural focus of intellectual dissent. The shock to a generation reared on the revolutionary conquests of Stalin and the Communist Party of the Soviet Union was no less profound than in the USSR itself, where many members of the same generation were deeply shaken by the revelations in Khrushchev's 'secret speech' to the Twentieth Party Congress in February 1956.

Iredyński did not set out to become a 'political' playwright and much of his writing, particularly his earlier writing and including the plays for radio presented here, deals with themes remote from the national crises noted above. Nevertheless his rebellious nature took shape against this background and may have been partly formed by these larger events. It found expression in scenes of shocking cruelty as well as verbal violence in his writing, particularly that for the stage. These he utilized in the presentation of themes which became increasingly daring in the context of 'People's Poland', the authoritarian

People's Republic of Poland, and sometimes presented a direct challenge to the communist authorities.

An early *succès de scandale* was *A Modern Nativity Play*, written in 1962 and permitted a brief stage run in Poznan in 1965 before being taken off. On the eve of the liberation of a concentration camp, the prisoners rehearse a nativity play in which Herod and the Holy Family are treated in a modern and metaphorical fashion. This play-within-a-play is the work of one of the camp guards. At one and the same time, the actors play themselves, characters from the traditional nativity play and their contemporary counterparts. The action takes place simultaneously on several different levels. One level of reality shows the concentration camp and a group of inmates who are ordered to enact a drama written by a guard. Another plane is represented by the Christmas mystery play, in which the conventional dramatic action becomes interwoven with the tragic lives of the abused and tortured actors who appear in it. This dimension of the drama constitutes the psychological plane, examining the relations between the characters and their theatrical embodiments. Yet another plane shows the guard – the author and the producer of the show – and his motivation for starting rehearsals on the eve of the liberation of the camp. All the actors who appear in the nativity play are to be killed, except the one who plays Herod and who, of all of them, is the most suspect morally. The guard's suicide crowns the entire masquerade. The borderline between the reality of the camp and the fictional enactment grows blurred. The guard, who is revealed to be the the camp commandant, is the true tyrant and executioner. Herod, an allegorical figure of tyranny from the mystery plays, becomes his theatrical embodiment and a modernized symbol of despotism. Herod – outside the camp a pimp and murderer – is the only one to survive and return to the outside world where he will continue to be a tyrant and wield power. A new terror yet awaits the world.

One of Iredyński's most powerful stage plays from the later period of his life, *An Altar Unto Himself* (1980), typifies the themes which preoccupied him at the peak of his career. In this play, Piotr M., a successful careerist, is seen reviewing his past and planning suicide, aided by numerous unwelcome spirits from his earlier life. We see his progress from high-minded youth in the 'forties to unscrupulous operator in middle age. He has learned how to survive and prosper in the communist system, gaining position by occasionally denouncing his friends, being active in the anti-semitic campaign of 1968 while keeping a Jewish mistress, and taking part in the suppression of the anti-government strikes and riots in Gdansk and Gdynia in 1970. Eventually, at the peak of a successful career his forgotten principles reassert themselves. While addressing a Party meeting he suddenly strips naked and declares that the naked truth must be shown. The ghosts from his past mock him pitilessly as he makes his suicide preparations.[5]

In this play Iredyński presents what has been termed 'a synthesis of the fate of Poland since 1945',[6] rich in specific allusions to key moments in that period which are instantly recognizable to a Polish audience. The picture is anything but heroic. The better instincts of those who at heart oppose the regime are easily neutralized.

There is a scene in *An Altar Unto Himself* in which Piotr M., in his capacity of censor of play-scripts, tells a promising young playwright that his play cannot be staged because it is 'too depressing'. Marc Robinson has pointed out that this could well apply to Iredyński's *Altar*,[7] but most of his other plays would also qualify.

Other late works, such as the play *Terrorists* published in 1982, confirmed yet again his place in what became known as the 'Theatre of Cruelty' and showed the *Galgenhumor* for which he became famous. Set in an unnamed Latin-American country and written at a time when Central America was seething with insurgency, the play depicts unscrupulous revolutionary leaders jockeying for position, seeking the best possible publicity in the mass media, murdering journalists in order to discredit the government side as murderers and willing to make martyrs of defecting comrades who have to be killed. Far from depicting the purity of the revolutionary cause, held up for admiration not only in socialist countries, it brings out the venality, corruption and expediency of all parties, and the Machiavellian nature of revolutionary politics.

Iredyński admitted to a single obsession: 'all my plays are about violence of one kind or another [...]. That is in the air. We carry it in ourselves.'[8] Accordingly he produced plays which seemed to be characterized by a disturbing ethical vacuum at their core, a world shorn of spiritual values and accepting no moral or religious authority. As Jan Kłossowicz once noted, his works may often be reduced, in essentials, to contests of strength, in which one side seeks to dominate, exploit or destroy the other.[9]

These plays also show the modern dramatic idiom which Iredyński had developed by this stage of his career. While distinctively his own, it draws on a variety of prominent novelists and playwrights of the twentieth century, above all its rebels and innovators. The names of Kafka, Sartre and Jean Genet are sometimes invoked.[10] There are similarities at times, especially in the radio plays, with Samuel Beckett.

When he deals with the social and political situation in modern Poland (as he does in *Altar*), those opposed to the totalitarian regime are easily corrupted, their moral sense corroded, whatever their original impulses may have been, to the extent that they are hardly superior morally to the evil oppressing them.

His depictions of the ruthlessness of life, the cruelty of human nature and cynical careerists might suggest a jaded and cynical view of life. Yet, while there is little authorial comment, an implicit judgement may be sensed behind the scenes so graphically presented to us. There are suggestions that hope of redemption is not altogether lost – Piotr M. does, after all, see the error of his ways – and more than a hint of humanity shines through at many points in his work. Iredyński did claim that his intentions were moralistic, though he might be 'un moraliste à rebours'.[11]

There were powerful messages in these plays for the Polish audience in the early 1980s, a time of unprecedented ferment as the totalitarian state was forced to loosen its grip under pressure from a disaffected population and work-force. Even when the state reasserted political control by force, imposing martial law in December 1981 and interning many leaders of anti-communist organizations, literature and the theatre could not be controlled to the same extent as they had been in earlier years. This was the time when Iredyński's major plays for the stage had their greatest impact.

Iredyński's plays for radio date from the period before Solidarity shook the communist regime to its foundations, a time of relative stability when overtly radical statements about the nature of society, of humanity and its predilection for violence could not easily be made publicly. In these short pieces the extremes of cruelty and brutal language are less in evidence, perhaps a reflection not only of the period but of the genre. The turbulence which marked his own life and the cruelty which characterizes so much of his other work, including his earlier stage plays, are not so apparent. We find ourselves in a relatively gentle world, in which people's dreams rather than their worst nightmares are explored.[12] Dreams, daydreams or people's secret aspirations play a prominent part in *The Radio*, *The Terrarium*, *First Prize*, *Nobody Dances Like That Now* and some of the other radio plays not included in this volume. Situations are kept simple, in keeping with the discipline imposed by the genre, which requires a single act or scene designed to be performed within a strict time limit of about half an hour. The theatrical technique is spare and economical. It relies almost entirely upon voice and language, with little or no help from sound effects or noises off. The cast is held to a minimum, often no more than two characters, between whom a conflict of some kind is usually played out, without the extremes of violence found in the stage plays.

Some of the plays for radio provide subtle studies in psychology and human relationships. One of them, *The Terrarium*, is overtly psychological, consisting of a conversation between a well-known actress in hospital after a suicide attempt and a young psychiatrist. She tries to give an account of her life and behaviour, indicating a wish to find an escape from the 'terrarium' in which she felt trapped, like the lizard she remembers from her childhood.

The other plays deal more specifically with relationships, in some cases new relationships just taking shape (*Nobody Dances Like That Now*), in others long-standing relationships (*The Window, The Radio, Ibis*); some freely selected (*Nobody Dances…*), others imposed by circumstances (*The Radio, Ibis*); some more or less comfortable (*Ibis*), others under strain (*The Kidnapping*). In some of the plays and the relationships depicted we may find strong elements of the theatre of the absurd. The author may, as was often his preference, give his plays no definite national setting and hold his focus firmly on personalities and human situations, or occasionally exploit elements of purely Polish social history, as he does in *Before the Lecture*. In the latter he interweaves into the story of the relationship between the two women a clear picture of broader developments throughout the post-war period.

The two protagonists have spent most of their adult lives as rivals for the affections of a weak-willed alcoholic poet, Marceli, to whom both have been married and who has since died. From their barbed conversation, at which Iredyński excels, it is clear that the ill feeling rankles no less than it did when Marceli was alive. There are hints at the traumas of post-war Poland. The power of the security police in the 'forties is clearly alluded to. The mention of one agent, Kielnicki, who lost his job in late 1956, is a direct reference to the changes in October of that year. The story of a triangular relationship emerges against a background of early post-war Poland, complete with tales of denunciation. The Librarian has served a prison term, having been arrested while the police sought her brother, a member of the anti-government resistance in the forest. She suspects the Speaker of denouncing her and her brother to the police. Marceli married first one then the other, but visited the first while married to the second, if (as it appears) the Librarian is telling the truth. Against this background, the story of the poet and his work, which the Speaker has come to tell, and which is likely to be in the adoring tradition then favoured in the communist world, must seem relatively pale and uninteresting. But Iredyński has his protagonist break with this tradition and open her public address with a swingeing attack on her old rival in love. At the this point the play ends.

Iredyński has a well-practised gift for maintaining dramatic tension in his dialogue and at giving his plays an unexpected twist at the end. This is clearly illustrated in *The Window*, in which nothing will shift the male protagonist from the window of his apartment, where he sits in the dark gazing at a window across the street, where the light of a match had briefly appeared a week earlier. He is unmoved by the anger and incomprehension of his female partner, who can only try to make sense of his behaviour by reading into it a more ordinary human impulse: had he seen a woman in the window? As their argument reaches fever pitch and serious domestic violence or marital breakdown seems inevitable (though Robert continues to observe the window opposite), the light flares again. He is immediately satisfied, his apparent obsessive interest passes at once and he is ready to resume normal social and family relations without further ado, but now his partner has seen something in the same window that sparks her interest.

There is more than a suggestion of the theatre of the absurd in this sort of circularity, which can also be seen in *Nobody Dances Like That Now*. With a light touch Iredyński guides the bantering dialogue of flirtation between Henryk and the much younger Maria, a university student, as they develop their acquaintanceship in his apartment, to the occasional accompaniment of the music he plays on his record-player. His attempt at casual seduction is at first resisted, but when she indicates a sexual interest of her own he reacts by merely wishing to master her more modern dancing style. The play ends where it began.

Ibis, which might well be considered the best of these plays, shares the circularity and the focus on a relationship, in this case clearly a long-established one. Stan and Hubert, veteran residents of a home for the aged, share an imagined private world in which an imaginary dog and imaginary visitors hold a central position. Their conversation is rich in allusions to their purely private world, which is impenetrable to outsiders. It is clear that a large part of their play-acting has been many times rehearsed. The newcomer to the home, unable to fathom their eccentric behaviour and their determined disregard for his presence, naturally assumes that these are directed against him or that they are symptoms of senile dementia. It emerges at the end, however, that the play has more to do with the relationship between the two and the power of a creative imagination to make life tolerable.

In both *The Radio* and *First Prize* the radio itself has an important function. It provides the focus through which the day-dreams or fantasies of the characters are variously expressed and destroyed. The winning lottery numbers, on which so much hope depends in *First Prize*, are read out over the radio. In the play entitled *The Radio*, a musical request programme is the vehicle via which the orphan Olo's imagined family is shown to be no more than his private fantasy. Both plays illustrate the foundering of illusions and hopes for change, but at the same time show that the relationships in which both pairs of characters appear to be trapped are fundamental to their existence and provide a firm basis, in spite of the antagonism that characterizes those relationships. Olo and

Bodzio, condemned to each other's company in a ward for the seriously ill, are unexpectedly shown to be very close. Tolek and Marcysia, the elderly couple similarly condemned in *First Prize*, are also closer than their verbal sparring at the beginning suggests, indeed bound by a perverse kind of devotion. It is difficult to imagine either having a meaningful life without the other, as in the case of Olo and Bodzio.

These plays represent only a small fraction of Ireneusz Iredyński's large output and can only convey a partial impression of his art. At the same time, however, they do display in compact form some of its salient features. His ability to create characters and sketch out relationships, his imaginative flair, his economy and skill with dialogue are all clearly evident. These are among the characteristics of the larger genres in which he made his mark. Although his career was tragically cut short, he was prolific enough in the time that he had to make a lasting contribution to his country's theatrical repertoire and to say much about his fellow-countrymen at this period of Poland's history. He may have appeared immodest when shortly before his death he placed himself in the same class as Sławomir Mrożek and Tadeusz Różewicz.[13] It is likely, however, that posterity will not disagree.

Note on the Translations

The following plays were jointly translated by Wojciech Dąbrowski and Kevin Windle:

Before the Lecture,
The Radio,
Nobody Dances Like That Now.

The remaining plays,

Ibis,
The Terrarium,
First Prize,
The Window,
The Kidnapping,
The Garden Gate,
and *Quadraphony,*
were translated by Kevin Windle.

The translators have sought to produce versions suitable for performance in English, whether on stage or radio, by an English-speaking cast.

For this reason, some of the more difficult Polish names have been replaced by approximate English equivalents, for example 'Staś' (short for 'Stanisław') by 'Stan', and 'Zosia' by 'Sophie'. In the text of the plays – as opposed to the Introduction – Polish proper names appear without their diacritical marks, as it is assumed that most of these will have little meaning for English-speaking performers.

The translators and the publisher are grateful to Mrs Teresa Iredyńska for permission to publish these English versions in the *Routledge Harwood Polish and East European Theatre Archive.*

All enquiries concerning performance rights should be addressed to: Samuel French, 45 West 25th Street, New York, NY 10010, USA.

Kevin Windle

1 Maria L. Danilewicz, *The Year's Work in Modern Language Studies*, XXIV, 1962, p. 544.
2 Elżbieta Baniewicz, 'New Productions', *The Theatre in Poland*, 5 (297), 1983, p. 15.
3 Jan Kłossowicz, 'Iredyński: męczeństwo z przymiarką', *Dialog*, 32/6 (1987), p. 114.
4 Andrzej Drawicz, *Wczasy pod lufą*, Warsaw, 1997, p. 13.
5 A valuable analysis in English of this play may be found in Marc Robinson, 'Ireneusz Iredyński's Drama of Exposure', *Modern Drama*, XXXII, No. 3 (1989), pp. 356–373. A slightly different version of this article, in Polish, was published as 'Iredyńskiego dramaty języka', *Dialog*, 33/3 (1988), pp. 117–127 (translated by Danuta Kuźnicka).
6 Lesław Eustachiewicz, *Dramaturgia współczesna*, 1945–1980, Warsaw, 1985, p. 343.
7 Marc Robinson, 'Ireneusz Iredyński's Drama of Exposure', *Modern Drama*, XXXII, No. 3 (1989), p. 368.
8 Kłossowicz, p. 117. Also quoted in Baniewicz, p. 8. The Polish word 'przemoc' may be translated as either 'violence' or 'coercion'.
9 Kłossowicz, p. 117.
10 References to these writers and others will be found in e.g. Kłossowicz, Eustachiewicz and Robinson.
11 Sława Bardijewska, 'Portraits d'auteurs dramatiques polonais: Le moralisme pervers d'Ireneusz Iredynski', *The Theatre in Poland*, 5 (297), 1983, p. 3.
12 Witold Billip comments on this gentler face of Iredyński in his Afterword to Ireneusz Iredyński, *Skąd ta wrazliwość*, Warsaw, 1979, p. 200.
13 Kłossowicz, p. 112.

IBIS

FIRST MAN: Where's that dog of mine? Ah, there you are, you rascal… *(Affectionately)* Come out of your corner, come on… That's the way, good doggy, good boy. Ibis, don't wipe your nose on my trousers. You mustn't. Lie down. Down… Stay. Good boy, good boy.

SECOND MAN: Nice dog, don't you think, Lavinia? Your average punter might take him for a mongrel, but actually he's a very special breed. The head of a Bavarian bearded shepherd, the body of a fleecy sheep, and the devil of a fine tail. You see that splendid tail, Lavinia? And those paws. Matching pairs of paws: the forepaws of a goat and the hind paws of Newfoundland. And such an unusual name – Ibis, the sacred bird of the ancient Egyptians. My friend here named him in a flash of inspiration. Stan, tell my dear lady-friend here how it happened.

FIRST MAN: I'll be glad to… The first time I saw this dog, ma'am, he was in a refuge for homeless animals. He was standing on one hind paw, with his forepaws on the mesh of his cage. He was holding up his other hind paw, with the claws turned down… Like an ibis, I thought, standing on one leg. I corrected myself at once: like a stork… But some hidden power told me I was right the first time. He became 'Ibis'. Doggie, we're not talking to you, we're talking about you, so don't get up. Down! That's the way… Good doggie.

NEW RESIDENT: Would you gents like some coffee? I've got a tin of instant.

(Silence)

NEW RESIDENT: All right.

(A moment's silence)

SECOND MAN: You must admit, Lavinia, that you don't see such a splendid animal every day.

(A moment's silence)

FIRST MAN: I'm so glad you like my dog, ma'am.

SECOND MAN: You can stroke him if you like, Lavinia. He's an unusually gentle dog… With the right people, of course… People like you, Lavinia.

FIRST MAN: Listen to him purring, the rascal… He likes you stroking him.

SECOND MAN: Mind that nice dress. Ibis might accidentally catch his claws on it.

NEW RESIDENT: *(his voice strained, almost shouting)* Cut it out, will you! That's enough! This really is the limit!

FIRST MAN: Steady, Ibis, steady. Down.

NEW RESIDENT: This is supposed to be a home for the aged!

SECOND MAN: Would you care for some herbal liqueur, Lavinia?

(A moment's silence)

SECOND MAN: My very own brew, of course.

FIRST MAN: In this glass you'll like it even better.

(Clink of glass)

SECOND MAN: No, you're wrong there, Lavinia. It isn't renaissance Murano. It dates from much later. That glass is no more than a hundred years old… A hundred and fifty at the outside.

NEW RESIDENT: Mad. Mad as hatters. They drink water out of mustard jars and say the mustard jars are antique – plain little jars made of ordinary glass.

FIRST MAN: How very true, ma'am. Hubert here is a real alchemist. His herbal liqueurs ought to be sold for their weight in gold.

SECOND MAN: Stan's being too kind, as usual. The drinks he makes are just as good if not better. That bitter wattleberry dewdrop of his, for example, is in a class of its own.

NEW RESIDENT: Talking to a non-existent woman, telling a non-existent dog to lie down! This is absolute lunacy!

FIRST MAN: No growling, Ibis. Mind your manners now.

SECOND MAN: As I said, my dear, that splendid animal is as gentle as a lamb, but only with the right people. Give him a whiff of some rogue passing the window and he'll voice his disapproval in that growling bass of his. Actually it's not so much a growl as a fragment of organ music.

NEW RESIDENT: How they keep up their refined chit-chat! Old pensioners just like me.

FIRST MAN: You should come to our little celebration tomorrow. Ibis is getting a new collar. We thought a gold chain would be in rather Byzantine taste, to put it mildly, so we chose a platinum one… Besides the collar, Ibis will get a marrow bone, while we fortify ourselves with champagne.

(A moment's silence)

SECOND MAN: You're quite sure? *(Pause)* What a pity, but never mind. We understand… In that case it'll be an exclusively male reception.

NEW RESIDENT: Reception! Reception! A bowl of soup with a bit of boiled beef – some reception! They can hardly afford cigarettes and they say they've bought the dog a platinum chain… home for the aged be damned! All for a non-existent dog!

FIRST MAN: We'd be glad to keep you company but unfortunately we have a meeting with Professor Stetski. The Professor's bringing some illustrative material for the book Hubert's working on.

SECOND MAN: *(after pause)* Lavinia, you're as charming as ever… Look, even Ibis is paying his tribute. Ibis boy, you bow most elegantly.

NEW RESIDENT: *(mimicking)* … 'the book Hubert's working on.' *(Angrily)* He cuts obituaries out of the newspaper and pastes them into a notebook, the fruitcake!

FIRST MAN: Goodbye, madam. I kiss your hand.

SECOND MAN: Goodbye, Lavinia. We've enjoyed your visit. You brought us sunshine and laughter.

(Footsteps. The sound of a door opening and closing. More footsteps)

FIRST MAN: Enchanting.

SECOND MAN: Such graceful movements.

NEW RESIDENT: Won't you gentlemen put yourselves in my position?

(Silence)

NEW RESIDENT: So you don't want to talk to me. All right. I can understand that. I'm new. I was admitted only three days ago. I might be in your way. I can understand all that. But why for pity's sake do you want to drive me to a madhouse? I can see through you. You're perfectly normal. You're just pretending. That non-existent dog and those non-existent people you carry on your stupid conversations with – it's all aimed at me… Can't you drop it now? You've had your fun at my expense, so now maybe we can start behaving normally. Can't we?

(Silence)

NEW RESIDENT: If you don't want to talk, don't. That's all right. But for Christ's sake cut out this loony play-acting! Do you want me to go right off my chump? I can't stay out of the room all day. It's too cold in the garden and you can only sit in the club-room till evening.. And it's evening now. What am I supposed to do?

(A moment's silence)

SECOND MAN: Stan, don't you think Ibis looks thirsty?

FIRST MAN: Yes, he's had nothing to drink all afternoon. I'll give him some water right away.

(Footsteps. Sound of water being poured into a bowl. Footsteps, the tap of a bowl on the floor)

FIRST MAN: Here, Ibis, drink.

(Lapping sound)

NEW RESIDENT: Which of you is lapping?

(Silence)

FIRST MAN: Thank you, Hubert, for reminding me. He really was thirsty. He's drunk almost a whole bowlful.

SECOND MAN: Perhaps we should ease our own parched throats as well.

FIRST MAN: I'll be only to too glad to.

SECOND MAN: To the lost continents of Atlantis and Mu!

FIRST MAN: Leaving out Lemuria?

SECOND MAN: We obviously can't drink to something that never existed.

FIRST MAN: Something that's a figment of a deranged imagination.

NEW RESIDENT: Look, instead of drinking water, have some coffee. I've got a whole tin of instant.

(Silence)

NEW RESIDENT: I know, at our age we shouldn't be drinking coffee at bedtime. You're right there, I admit… Yes, you're right. But a glass of real cognac won't do us any harm. Cognac boosts the circulation and when you have some at bedtime you go to sleep faster. You don't believe I have any? But I have. Here, look! And glasses for it too. Just the right type. Brandy glasses. You hold the glass in your palm, the cognac warms up and the bouquet rises. Well, how about it?

FIRST MAN: Lemuria, Hubert, is a figment of a deranged imagination.

SECOND MAN: Unlike Atlantis and the continent of Mu.

FIRST MAN: I drink to the splendour of lost civilizations.

SECOND MAN: A civilization swallowed up by the Atlantic and another sunk in the Pacific.

NEW RESIDENT: If you don't want to drink my cognac you can drink your own water and eat bread with it. I'll drink my cognac myself. There, see? I sniff it: what a lovely aroma! And now a swig, straight from the bottle. Lovely!

FIRST MAN: Would you care for a bit of caviar, Hubert?

SECOND MAN: That'd be nice, Stan.

FIRST MAN: Black caviar or grey?
SECOND MAN: I prefer Persian.
FIRST MAN: Grey then.

(A moment's silence)

SECOND MAN: You can't beat Persian caviar.

FIRST MAN: You're behind the times, Hubert. These days it's called Iranian.

SECOND MAN: I had a classical education so let me use the ancient name… Anyway the Greeks had never heard of Iran, but they had heard of Persia.

NEW RESIDENT: Old men chewing on some old lozenges and saying they're eating caviar.

FIRST MAN: Speaking of the Greeks, did you know, Hubert, that in my youth I often dreamed of Xenophon's 'Retreat of the Ten Thousand'? That truly is splendid prose.

SECOND MAN: Dreams like that can have a Freudian interpretation.

FIRST MAN: *(laughing)* So you suppose those ten thousand…

SECOND MAN: *(also laughing)* I'm sure of it, Stan. I'm almost sure of it.

NEW RESIDENT: You've got ten thousand white mice in your addled brains, or ten thousand bats in the belfry… To hell with the pair of you! I'll have another drink. You can have your lozenges and water. I'll have some cognac.

FIRST MAN: Isn't Lavinia just made for Chanel?

SECOND MAN: You're right there, Stan. That dress is lovely.

FIRST MAN: Ibis came close to tearing it with his claws.

SECOND MAN: She'd have forgiven him. Lavinia can tell if someone does something crazy out of love, and she can appreciate that.

FIRST MAN: Do you hear that, Ibis? Look at him stretching! He understands everything.

NEW RESIDENT: I know you'd like to have a dog. But they aren't allowed here and never will be. They'd cause trouble and get in people's way. You'll never have a dog.

SECOND MAN: Stan, don't you think Ibis has been scratching a lot lately?

FIRST MAN: Are you wondering if…

SECOND MAN: Well, you know how it is: to err is human, to have fleas canine.

FIRST MAN: We'll have to give him a bath tomorrow with insecticidal shampoo.

SECOND MAN: Did you see him shudder? He doesn't like those baths one little bit.

FIRST MAN: He understands everything you say, the rascal.

NEW RESIDENT: *(slightly tipsy)* That dog stinks. I won't stand for it. This is a room for three people. People only. People, do you hear? We'll have no smelly dogs in it. There's no place for livestock in a home for the aged!

(Growl)

NEW RESIDENT: Which of you growled?

(Silence)

NEW RESIDENT: You drivelling old dotards! You clowning idiots! There's no dog here. I made a joke but you don't even understand jokes! You just keep on with your bloody play-acting!

FIRST MAN: After his bath tomorrow, with his platinum chain on, Ibis will look really dignified.

SECOND MAN: He doesn't look too pleased now.

FIRST MAN: He's yawning in protest... Don't worry, Ibis, don't you worry. Go back to bed.

SECOND MAN: Lazy beast. Look how slowly he walks.

FIRST MAN: He's not as young as he was, Hubert.

SECOND MAN: A woolly beast in his prime.

NEW RESIDENT: The smarmy way they babble on, the old buggers. Feeding each other's fantasies.

FIRST MAN: Look, Hubert, he's put his head on the pillow again. I wouldn't be surprised if one day he started talking.

SECOND MAN: I wonder what his first words would be.

FIRST MAN: I hope he wouldn't find anything to reproach us for.

SECOND MAN: We've done nothing to deserve that, Stanley.

FIRST MAN: I quite agree, but you never know. Ibis might think his walks have been too short.

SECOND MAN: A dog that could start talking should have enough brains to realize that we're not up to long walks at our age.

FIRST MAN: I reckon Ibis would be glad to recite some passage from 'Les Fleurs du mal' for Lavinia.

SECOND MAN: Stan, judging by the face he's making, you have to admit he'd be happier reeling off some good old-fashioned bawdy.

FIRST MAN: You're probably right, Hubert... He does look have the look of an old pervert.

NEW RESIDENT: It's no good pretending! You live like a pair of old beggars and you'll die like beggars. And that won't be long. You'll cark and I'll watch. I'm younger than you. You'll go to the grave before me. I know how old you are. I asked who I'd be sharing with. They told me... They lied. They said there were these two nice cultivated gentlemen... And what do I find? Two soft-headed human wrecks! I don't give a fig about you. You might as well not exist. You can go and talk to a whale. What do I care? I've got my cognac, and in the daytime I'll find myself some normal people for company.

FIRST MAN: I don't think Lavinia would mind hearing a few dirty words from Ibis, Hubert.

SECOND MAN: She wouldn't be cross. She'd be amused.

FIRST MAN: Ibis must be having a nightmare. He's waving his paws as if he was pushing somebody away.

SECOND MAN: Maybe he's running over some lush emerald-green meadow.

FIRST MAN: Let's hope so.

(Squeal)

SECOND MAN: He yelped.

FIRST MAN: Yes, I heard. Wake up, Ibis, wake up, doggy! Everything's all right – you've got your friends, your security… No need for any bad dreams. Good dog, good dog.

SECOND MAN: He agrees… Look, Stan, he's wagging his tail.

NEW RESIDENT: How long can you keep this up? You want to wear me down, do you? You won't. You're too feeble. Better men than you have tried it. I always come out on top. You won't be here long. You belong on a funny farm, not in a home for the aged. I'll write a letter and an ambulance will come and take you away. And I'll stand in the window and blow you kisses. In the meantime I'll have a drink. Good riddance!

FIRST MAN: Don't you think it's about time for a change of medicine, Hubert?

SECOND MAN: Do you think we ought to move on to your bitter brew?

FIRST MAN: Stout fellow! You've said it! Time for a drop of the wattleberry dew!

NEW RESIDENT: Putting drops of valerian into water and calling it 'wattleberry dew'! Stupid old buggers!

SECOND MAN: A splendid drink.

FIRST MAN: I prefer the liqueurs you make.

SECOND MAN: Look, Stan. Ibis is smiling.

FIRST MAN: How sweetly he sleeps. Paws up in the air, head on one side, and that blissful smile.

NEW RESIDENT: Dogs don't smile. Only humans can smile. And some monkeys.

SECOND MAN: Now I'm sure he's running over a lush emerald-green meadow.

FIRST MAN: Sniffing at those tempting scents on the molehills.

SECOND MAN: Perhaps in a moment he'll meet some enchanting russet-coloured female... Haven't anything against Irish setters, have you, Stan?
FIRST MAN: I'm all for them... The offspring would be a marvellous mixture.
NEW RESIDENT: Why do you go on like this? Why? What have I done to you? Am I any different? Don't I eat, sleep and breathe? Aren't I just as lonely as you? Answer me!

(Silence)

NEW RESIDENT: *(shouting)* Put the light out! It's my bedtime!
FIRST MAN: I think perhaps we should spare Ibis his encounter with that insecticidal shampoo tomorrow.
SECOND MAN: You're right. Let's not spoil his mood on such a splendid occasion. We'll give him his bath the day after tomorrow.
FIRST MAN: The rascal sends his thanks.
SECOND MAN: Did you really have dreams about 'The Retreat of the Ten Thousand'?
FIRST MAN: I had a teacher who had had an unhappy personal life and admired people of the stature of Xenophon.
SECOND MAN: I see.
NEW RESIDENT: And I don't see! Nobody in his right mind could understand all this bloody make-believe! Where do you think you're living? What do you get out of this? Your play-acting doesn't change anything? You're a pair of old derelicts taken into a home for the aged out of charity and no amount of make-believe will alter that... How beautiful this cognac looks against the light! Look, it's like gold...
FIRST MAN: Professor Stetski's a bit late.
SECOND MAN: He's famous for being absent-minded, Stan. But I'm sure he'll come.
FIRST MAN: Where did he get those photos of the ruins of those monumental structures on those Pacific islands?
SECOND MAN: Professor Sutherland of Oxford sent them to him.
FIRST MAN: Oh, is that so?
NEW RESIDENT: Poxford, not Oxford, you grubby old gaffers!
FIRST MAN: Then let's drink a drop to the lost civilizations.
SECOND MAN: To Atlantis and the continent of Mu!
NEW RESIDENT: You could have a wash instead. Take a look at yourselves in the mirror. See what you look like! Grey stubble on your cheeks, crud on your collars, ugh! 'Cultivated gentlemen', they said! Dirty old dead-beats!

FIRST MAN: You know, that saying of Professor Stetski's always makes me laugh. I wonder if he used it in the past. If you said it to a woman in an intimate situation it might be slightly shocking, mightn't it?

SECOND MAN: *(laughing)* Stan, Stan!...

NEW RESIDENT: That's enough! Stop! Say something to me! Challenge me! Let's have this out like real, normal people. I know you're putting it on. You're normal. You just want to finish me off! Say something to me!

FIRST MAN: Look, Hubert. Ibis has turned onto his side.

SECOND MAN: He's scratching his ear.

NEW RESIDENT: No! No! A hundred times no! That's enough! I'm leaving! I'm going to the manager! He can put me wherever he likes for the night! I won't stay with you! You're lower than dirt! *(In a voice verging on hysteria)* You ghoulish monsters! *(Shouting)* Monsters!

(Footsteps, doors slamming. A moment of silence)

SECOND MAN: So what now?

FIRST MAN: *(gently)* We have a dog... His name's Ibis.

BEFORE THE LECTURE

FEMALE LIBRARIAN: Good afternoon. I'm so glad you were willing to come to a boring little town like ours and I can assure you our modest library will be packed to capacity for your talk. People here are curious about living legends, and television can't give them what they want. It's one thing to have an image on the screen and quite another to have a living person in front of you.

INVITED FEMALE SPEAKER: *(astonished)* So it's you, is it?

LIBRARIAN: *(dropping formal tone)* Yes, it's me… Take a seat. Here I am receiving you in this office when I ought to have been waiting out there on the library steps… *(sarcastically)* to give you the red carpet treatment… But as you see, I've got this cast on my leg. When you reach my age the most exciting thing you can look forward to is a fall down the stairs… Oh, I'm speaking for myself of course – you look so much younger.

SPEAKER: I *am* younger. Three years younger.

LIBRARIAN: Smooth neck, firm cheeks… Do you tell your surgeon he's got magnetic hands too?

SPEAKER: No, I just pay him.

LIBRARIAN: Oh, he must be ugly… Make yourself comfortable… How about some coffee? You've still got half an hour before you start.

SPEAKER: I don't drink coffee these days.

LIBRARIAN: Of course. You were ever so sensible in *those* days too.

SPEAKER: Why didn't you put your signature on the invitation, if you're in charge of the library?

LIBRARIAN: Of our little 'cultural centre'? We have a library, a reading room, an activities centre and a small lecture hall.

SPEAKER: Did you think I wouldn't come if I saw your signature?

LIBRARIAN: You probably wouldn't have. And I wanted to see you… Anyway I was in hospital, because of my leg… My deputy signed for me. She's a nice girl, don't you think?

SPEAKER: Have you told her anything about us? She gave me an odd look.

LIBRARIAN: Don't be silly… She's just like any other little provincial girl who's eager to learn about the big city.

SPEAKER: *(absent-mindedly)* I suppose so... *(Metallically)* Do you want something from me?

LIBRARIAN: Do you mean some sort of reward, or sponsorship in the capital?

SPEAKER: Something like that.

LIBRARIAN: No. I've got everything I need here. A little house with a garden, good friends, respect, popularity. And don't forget, I retire in a year.

SPEAKER: Are you telling me you simply wanted to see me? Is that all?

LIBRARIAN: What's so funny about that? We've known each other for ages, and the mere fact that we haven't seen each other for so long doesn't change my attitude to you in the slightest.

SPEAKER: You hate me.

LIBRARIAN: Rubbish.

SPEAKER: You used to hate me once.

LIBRARIAN: I've just told you I have exactly the same attitude to you now as I had then, and it's not hatred – just amazement that people like you exist.

SPEAKER: You feel you're better than me?

LIBRARIAN: No. Just different.

SPEAKER: What do you want?

LIBRARIAN: To talk to you... To ask you one or two questions.

SPEAKER: Such as?

LIBRARIAN: How did Marceli die?

SPEAKER: It took several days, but he was in a coma... He didn't suffer. He died at night, that is, about four in the morning.

LIBRARIAN: Were you with him?

SPEAKER: No. I'd gone home to catch some sleep.

LIBRARIAN: Then I gather you'd stayed at his bedside up till then, and everybody felt sorry for you.

SPEAKER: Is that so strange? I was his wife.

LIBRARIAN: Yes, and now you're his widow. The grieving widow. And the title of your talk is 'My husband's life and work.'

SPEAKER: Do you hold it against me?

LIBRARIAN: Not at all. It's a fine thing you're doing, keeping alive the memory of a marvellous artist... Oh, how lucky I remembered... Sign here that you've received your fee... There, and here's your money. *(Pause)* You haven't counted it.

SPEAKER: If that's supposed to be cutting I don't think much of it.

LIBRARIAN: We're most particular about these things here in the backwoods. And besides, I wouldn't like to have you suspect me of anything again.

SPEAKER: You believed the gossip spread by that major of State Security who lost his post after the changes in 1956. Don't you realize he wanted to be some character out of Shakespeare, not just a policeman abusing his power? That's why he dreamed up all those melodramas, making out people had done all sorts of things. He used to tell his stories to anyone who'd stand him a drink. He went to pieces mentally when he came out of prison.

LIBRARIAN: That's the first I've heard about any major.

SPEAKER: I mean Kielnicki.

LIBRARIAN: Oh, you mean old Ziutek! Remember how you called him Ziutek as soon as you met him? I didn't know he'd joined State Security. In the 'forties, when he was in Lodz, he was a journalist.

SPEAKER: He was transferred later.

LIBRARIAN: I see… Lodz, a lovely evening. In June 1947. Marceli and I were having a marvellous time. You came and sat down, a slip of a girl, so shy and charming, looking a little bit lost. Then along came Ziutek with some of his friends. You obviously needed somebody to protect you, so all the men made a fuss of you, the way they always did. Then Ziutek saw you home. You gave him your pure innocent look and said 'Ziutek' so nicely.

SPEAKER: *(after a pause)* Will I have a microphone?

LIBRARIAN: No, the hall isn't very big… While we're on the subject of your lecture, I hear the post-graduate student who wrote it for you is a nice-looking boy, and his doctoral thesis is about Marceli.

SPEAKER: The text is my own.

LIBRARIAN: Of course, since you're presenting it… Do you remember those sweet little verses of yours that so enchanted Marceli? Wasn't it that funny little poet with the turned-up nose who wrote them for you? But you told Marceli they were your own and published them as yours. That is, Marceli got them published… Such a touching idea – spending a night with a poet and charging him a couple of poems instead of money. And you never know – in the long term, and of course in a very few cases, it might be more profitable.

SPEAKER: He gave them to me. I was young. I was surrounded by celebrities and wanted to do something to keep up with them, so I said I'd written them myself… But to you, as my friend, I admitted everything.

LIBRARIAN: You're pretty little face never fooled me. I knew right away that you weren't up to writing verses like that, so when I put the screws on during a little heart-to-heart you owned up. But don't forget, I didn't tell Marceli. In other words I put my loyalty to you above my loyalty as a wife… I don't know if you remember, but I was Marceli's wife at the time.

SPEAKER: My talk about Marceli is my own work though… *(Giggling)* I did learn a bit in all those years.

LIBRARIAN: I believe you on both counts… I used to like your visits, you know… You used to amaze me… You knew exactly what you wanted… You were one of the very few girls in those circles at that time who didn't drink or smoke, tried not to keep too many late nights and sought the right friends. Cold as ice. But the men didn't notice that, or most of them didn't. Marceli was so comically infatuated with you. He sometimes called you his poor little cherub and I never added that, while his poor little cherub hadn't much verbal intelligence, she had the intelligence of a predator. I didn't foresee any threat from you, although the cherub had nice curves and long legs. I had what it takes myself, and I was sure of Marceli's love.

SPEAKER: Yes, you were sure of yourself all right. Very sure.

LIBRARIAN: So were you. But you wore a mask.

SPEAKER: I was just learning to.

LIBRARIAN: Was your plan to eliminate me from Marceli's life an improvisation, or had you some suspicions that you wanted confirmed?

SPEAKER: What makes you think I was the one who informed on you? They must have been on your brother's trail, and that's why you were arrested.

LIBRARIAN: Now you listen to me. Our house was your second home. You were with us, or in our house, every day. And one day you see a young man turning up unexpectedly, behaving rather wildly, and you put two and two together. When his jacket is unbuttoned you can see he has a gun, and that reminds you of Marceli's tirades about my stupid brother who's out in the forest with the anti-government resistance. You go out. Marceli's down at the café. You say you have a date there too and give me to understand you don't want to be in the way while my brother's there. Twenty minutes later there's a knock at the door. My fool of a brother uses his gun and jumps out of the window, and they arrest me.

SPEAKER: Even if I had informed, I'd have been doing the right thing. Historically and morally.

LIBRARIAN: Don't talk to me about morality. Are you trying to tell me you were obliged to inform because of your convictions?

SPEAKER: Suppose I am.

LIBRARIAN: You had no convictions whatever, my dear. You were utterly bereft of any political beliefs. You went after the strong, the people who could make life easier for you. If the political situation had been different you would have had just as much admiration for people with quite opposite views, as long as they had just one thing in their favour: power.

SPEAKER: Even in a godforsaken place like this you manage to feel superior.

LIBRARIAN: Heavens! The sarcasm! It wouldn't have been so bad if you'd actually loved Marceli.

SPEAKER: What makes you so sure I didn't?

LIBRARIAN: I know what happened afterwards, just a short time afterwards.

SPEAKER: I married him.

LIBRARIAN: The fact that he got a divorce from a wife who was in prison was in a way a result of the overall situation, the climate of the times. That I can accept. But your pushing him on into ever uglier alliances of ambition, and clearing the path with your body – was that supposed to be love? After you moved to Warsaw you passed through so many beds that you'll forgive me for not believing in the nobility of your motives. I could put it in one short word, but I'd rather not.

SPEAKER: He didn't waste time either.

LIBRARIAN: I know about that.

SPEAKER: How?

LIBRARIAN: He wrote to me, and came here to see me lots of times.

(A moment of silence.)

LIBRARIAN: He sought me out as soon as he heard I was out of prison.

SPEAKER: He did?

LIBRARIAN: Yes.

SPEAKER: And are those letters…

LIBRARIAN:… still in my possession? Yes. Several hundred of them. But don't worry. If they're ever published it won't be until you and I are dead and gone.

SPEAKER: Is there much about me in them?

LIBRARIAN: Not a great deal, but some nice comments… You see, he never blamed anybody else's actions for his own misfortunes. Although he was an alcoholic, he had greatness, which you couldn't appreciate. Never, even though you used to whisper that he had magnetic hands when he stroked your hair, back in our Lodz days.

SPEAKER: And when he came here he stayed with you.

LIBRARIAN: Yes. And if you can imagine it, he didn't drink. For some reason he didn't need to.

SPEAKER: You're lying. You haven't got those letters.

LIBRARIAN: I can show you one. Here you are. You can read it. Read it aloud, if you like. You'll recognize the writing.

(Silence.)

LIBRARIAN: Sure you wouldn't like some coffee now? You look a bit off colour.

SPEAKER: Stop talking about coffee. You invited me here to make a fool of me.

LIBRARIAN: Make a fool of you?

SPEAKER: In a little town like this, people are bound to remember him if he came here.

LIBRARIAN: Oh, is that what's bothering you? You've got nothing to worry about. He used to sit in the house for days on end, and my house is on the edge of town… Sometimes we went out for a walk, but only in the evenings, and only out into the fields… I had my reputation to think about… *(in a lower voice)* and his peace of mind.

SPEAKER: Maybe that's so… But I'm his widow.

LIBRARIAN: *(brightly)* People haven't forgotten me either, even though I reverted to my maiden name after the divorce… That post-graduate student, for instance, managed to find me… Perhaps it was just a cheap boast, that he'd written your talk. Young people do like to indulge their fantasies after a glass of brandy.

SPEAKER: Here. Take your money. I'm not giving any talk.

LIBRARIAN: In the first place, it's not my money, but a State fund, and in the second pace you can't disappoint the town's cultural élite. You're one thing to me, but something quite different to them. The Grand Lady, the Widow in Mourning of old, lamenting her fate, the Keeper of the Flame.

SPEAKER: You're right. Why should I waste my time and give up my fee for the sake of a psychopathic old woman? I'll give my lecture.

LIBRARIAN: Thank you… I was afraid you'd become sentimental.

SPEAKER: Don't you feel lonely here?

LIBRARIAN: I've told you: I have everything I need.

SPEAKER: You retire in a year. You might feel useless.

LIBRARIAN: There's not much danger of that.

SPEAKER: What would you say to the idea of moving to Warsaw and moving in with me? The flat's big enough now that Marceli's gone; we'd have …

(Librarian's laughter interrupts her.)

LIBRARIAN: Live together? What would we do? What would we talk about? The past? Marceli? That's all dead and gone.

SPEAKER: I had the impression it was all very much alive to you.

LIBRARIAN: You're the one who's alive to me. That's why I wanted to see you, but surely you don't think I want to turn my life into a soap opera?

SPEAKER: We're not that young any more. We might be able to help each other.

LIBRARIAN: We're both fairly independent.

SPEAKER: As you like. I was already picturing the two of us chatting merrily over afternoon tea, or holding bridge parties …

LIBRARIAN: No doubt everybody would talk about your generosity and high-mindedness, how you'd hauled Marceli's first wife out of that provincial backwater and taken her home to feed and clothe her. What a great-hearted woman!

SPEAKER: *(chuckling)* You still think I have only my own good at heart.

LIBRARIAN: Do you know what a black widow is?

SPEAKER: Yes, a horrible sort of spider… But I don't think Marceli would have approved of it as a metaphor for me. He would have said it wasn't 'dialectical' enough, not meaningful enough.

LIBRARIAN: Who knows whether he would have approved or not? He didn't like insects, and he loathed spiders.

SPEAKER: Then why didn't he leave me?

LIBRARIAN: He was probably too weak by then.

SPEAKER: *(thoughtfully)* He was always weak.

LIBRARIAN: Yes. In a sense.

SPEAKER: Would you believe me if I told you something in me burned up when I won him so quickly? That something in me burned up when he renounced you?

LIBRARIAN: I don't think so.

SPEAKER: You don't? But it did. I regarded you two as different from me, upright, and fine. I might be bad, I thought, but I knew you two were different, and better. I admired you both.

LIBRARIAN: You admired me, and therefore set about stealing my husband.

SPEAKER: I don't see any contradiction in that… You sometimes think in the logic of men.

LIBRARIAN: Funny sort of motivation you've found for living with Marceli. 'I was disloyal, mean and spiteful because he didn't measure up to my ideals.' In that case why didn't you divorce him?

SPEAKER: I felt at home with him. I got used to him. It made a lot of things easier.

LIBRARIAN: That's for sure… Would you take a peep through the door, my dear, and see if the hall's filled up yet? We ought to be going in.

(Footsteps, silence, more footsteps.)

SPEAKER: It's full. They're all dressed up to the nines.

LIBRARIAN: I told you, this is a great event for them.

SPEAKER: You've made this little office your inner sanctum. Nobody to come in and tell us it's time to begin.

LIBRARIAN: They come in when I invite them.

SPEAKER: I can see it really was silly of me to suggest you move in with me. There you'd be just another nice old lady, whereas here you're somebody, the arbiter of culture and good taste.

LIBRARIAN: Now that's enough of your compliments... You're right, I'm perfectly content with my life here.

SPEAKER: Did you often think you ought to kill me?

LIBRARIAN: Yes, often. Many years ago.

SPEAKER: I used to as well, and not so long ago.

LIBRARIAN: Think of killing me?

SPEAKER: Yes, killing you. To put it politely, I'd have been glad to hear you'd died. It would have been like having a corn removed from my consciousness.

LIBRARIAN: From your conscience, you mean.

SPEAKER: It makes no difference.

LIBRARIAN: *(after a pause)* Let's go. Give me my stick... Thank you... Should I introduce you or will you start by yourself?

SPEAKER: I'll start by myself. I'm used to it.

(Footsteps, a door opens. Background sound changes. Voices in conversation, which die down, applause, an expectant hush emphasized by a cough.)

SPEAKER: Good evening, ladies and gentlemen. This evening I was supposed to talk about my husband's life and work, but, having in mind the venue, I have decided to restrict myself to one matter only, a painful and tragic matter for my husband and me, which I would like to lay before you for you to judge... Before you, because among you, in your charming town lives the person who, having been Marceli's first wife, later became for him a source of pain, vexation and moral shame.

(Fade out.)

THE RADIO

BODZIO: What a Sunday! What a hell of a Sunday!… My lunch went down like barbed wire, the angels are peeing on this sinful world, and to cap it all the bloody radio's churning out this… I ought to smash this head-set on the floor and …

OLO: Go on and smash it.

BODZIO: Shut up, pipsqueak. I'm not talking to you.

OLO: Then who *are* you talking to? There's only two of us in this ward.

BODZIO: I'm talking to myself… What a hell of a Sunday… Some people have relatives visiting, and I have to sit and stare at that ugly mug… Oh, what's the use?… I swear to God I'll have to ask the doctor tomorrow to move me somewhere else. I can't bear having to look at Olo's ugly mug. A real pig's mug! If only I could spit on it, but the oaf's bed is too far away. Two years! Two whole years I've had to look at him! There's no justice!

OLO: Keep your hair on, grand-dad. If your family haven't come today something must have kept them. They'll come next week. Save your breath, Bodzio.

BODZIO: You don't have to worry about my breath. You'll be leaving this world before I do.

OLO: That's as maybe…

BODZIO: Not maybe. That's for sure. They'll take you down to the little building at the bottom of the grounds, slit you open like a pig, take a look inside, shove in some paper stuffing and sew you up again with two seams.

OLO: Why not five?

BODZIO: If I say two, pipsqueak, there'll be two.

OLO: Have it your own way, grand-dad.

BODZIO: *(dreamily)* Yes… Two seams… They'll dress you and tip you into a nasty little grave. Cheapest sort of coffin. Nobody there but the gravediggers. And they'll be drunk… Yes… A fine end. Not long now, Olo. It's getting closer all the time..

OLO: But maybe you'll go first, you old King Herod. You're pushing sixty, forty years older than me. You take precedence over me.

BODZIO: Have you forgotten how we drew lots on the terrace? Who drew first place?

OLO: I did.

BODZIO: That means you'll go first. That's the will of Fate. Besides, what sort of life does a chronic invalid have?... Do you want to go on suffering for decades to come? You ought to be glad you'll be first to go.

OLO: *(pause)* It was so nice on the terrace this morning... Sunny, with a light breeze.

BODZIO: When they put you in the ground the weather'll be just as foul as it is now. Drunken gravediggers, pelting rain, wet clay and water in the pit ...

OLO: My old man'll be there, and the old lady'll bring along at least three priests – she's very religious... And the old man'll see there's an orchestra, wreaths, flowers... That's how it'll be, grand-dad. I'll be buried in style.

BODZIO: Ha-ha! Hold on to me or I'll regain the use of my legs. From laughing. Whole family! The gall of the little bounder! Not even a lame dog for a visitor in two years, and he starts telling me about his mum and dad! If he'd even had a Christmas card from them... But no, nothing. Not a word. Nothing.

OLO: But they'll see I get a fine funeral. An orchestra, flowers ...

BODZIO: ... three priests, of course. And a bishop as well, I suppose.

OLO: No, there might not be a bishop.

BODZIO: Thank the Lord for that! I was beginning to wonder... I'll call the nurse.

OLO: You had the bed-pan just a moment ago, grandpa.

BODZIO: When I look at you my insides start turning over.

OLO: Then don't look.

BODZIO: Looking at that snout of yours gives me a pain, but it has its happier side too. The ones who look a picture of health are the ones who have a way of popping off from heart attacks. So I just wonder when that'll be.

OLO: Before you. Don't worry, before you.

BODZIO: I know that, but when?

OLO: Take your finger off that bell. She'll come soon enough.

BODZIO: Why are you sticking up for her? Because she's young, like you? So what if she is? She's got no heart.

OLO: And would you have any heart for people like us, grandpa? Bathing us, giving us the bed-pan, lifting us into wheelchairs ...

BODZIO: She turns me over like a log and scrubs me as if I had sheet-iron instead of skin.

OLO: So she ought. And she ought to box your ears every time as well.
BODZIO: You snake!
OLO: Talking to me?
BODZIO: Who else?
OLO: Take your finger off that bell.
BODZIO: I won't take it off. What's she up to? On the phone to some rutting stud, I suppose, and we can all drop dead... I bet she's a real bed-hopper, I've got an eye for these things.
OLO: You've got a jaundiced eye.
BODZIO: She's a slut.

(Sound of door opening; footsteps)

NURSE: Beds on fire, gentlemen, or something? Who wants the bed-pan?
BODZIO: Nobody, nurse. My, you do look pretty today! Bright-eyed and rosy-cheeked. Milk and roses!
NURSE: What do you want, Bodzio?
BODZIO: Well, you see, nurse ...
NURSE: Be quick, Bodzio. I have to run to Ward Six. They're ringing from there too.
BODZIO: The radio's not working. Not a peep out of the headphones. I expect old Wolski at the relay station's gone to sleep, the old drunkard... Maybe you could phone him and tell him to put something on, so we needn't get bored.
NURSE: I see... I can't do anything. Other people have been complaining too. I rang the station. Something's gone wrong, some cable or something. They can't fix it till tomorrow.
BODZIO: *(shouting)* But I have to listen to the radio today! So has he. Isn't that right, Olo?
OLO: We'll get by without it today, Bodzio... We'll have a chat instead.
BODZIO: *(still shouting)* Idiot! I want to listen to the radio today!
NURSE: What's wrong with you, Bodzio? You're always so polite.
BODZIO: I'm not today and that's all there is to it. Full stop! *(Shouting)* I must listen to it today. This minute!
NURSE: What can I do? Oh... Hold on ...
BODZIO: *(ingratiatingly)* I knew you'd come up with something, nurse.
NURSE: I'll bring you a little set from the doctors' common room, an ordinary one, without headphones... If it won't bother you, Olo.
OLO: No, I'd like to listen too.
BODZIO: You're an angel, nurse... An angel with lovely curves.
NURSE: Steady, Bodzio, or your blood pressure will shoot up.

(Footsteps, sound of door closing)

BODZIO: *(hissing)* Slut!
OLO: Come off it, grandpa! Just a nice bit of crumpet.
BODZIO: That's just it. *Too* nice. They shouldn't hire women like that. Bad for the nerves.
OLO: You still interested in women, Bodzio?
BODZIO: None of your business, pipsqueak. Anyway I'm not talking to you.
OLO: Who are you talking to?
BODZIO: Myself.
OLO: Then I'm sorry, King Herod.
BODZIO: You …
OLO: Talking to me?
BODZIO: No, to myself.
OLO: Eh?
BODZIO: Something tells me you're still innocent. Sticking up for dames the way you do… At least I've got it all behind me… While you haven't ever made it, poor little bugger.
OLO: Do you expect me to tell you all about it?
BODZIO: You only know about those things from books.
OLO: Oh yes? Then you can go and read some books yourself. I won't tell you anything.
BODZIO: What are you so cross about, my poor little bugger?
OLO: I thought you weren't going to talk to me.
BODZIO: True… Tomorrow I'll tell the doctor to move you out. Yes, kindly remove Olo, the vile pipsqueak. Enough is enough. All of two years I've had to stare at his ugly mug. And he doesn't even show any respect for my grey hair.
OLO: You've only got a bit of grey hair left at the sides, baldpate.
BODZIO: He'll have to go. I'll stay here; I've got used to this room. But Olo must go.
OLO: I wonder what my old man's doing now. Probably taken the car and gone off into the country… Enjoying a long *fin de semaine* …
BODZIO: A long what?
OLO: A long *fin de semaine.*
BODZIO: Short fantasies are better for you.
OLO: He's probably in bed with some cracker of a girl… Not so young any more but he still pulls the women. Natural enough, I suppose, when you're a big name.
BODZIO: You mean your mum lets him.
OLO: She's resigned to it. Being married to a great man isn't easy. So what can she do? She wouldn't go and divorce him… She stays at home

and reads or watches TV. In the evening she goes to church, meets one of her friends afterwards …

BODZIO: Then perhaps you can explain to me why, if your mother's so religious …

OLO: More than religious, Bodzio, she's a religious maniac… I reckon it's her revenge for a failed marriage… It's a refuge for her. Bodzio. She thought married life would be something different …

BODZIO: If she's so religious, why doesn't she show some interest in her little lad and visit him once a year at least?

OLO: I've forbidden her.

BODZIO: She could still write to you.

OLO: I've forbidden her to write.

BODZIO: Why?

OLO: My life is here. I don't want any more to do with that life. They understand that.

BODZIO: Funny sort of understanding.

OLO: Nothing funny about it, grandpa. No recollections, no news of what's happening there.

BODZIO: But you listen to the radio.

OLO: That tells me about the world. My family isn't the world.

BODZIO: *(after a pause)* It's raining even harder… What a hell of a Sunday… It'll be an hour before Sophie brings that radio, I can tell you.

OLO: You talking to me?

BODZIO: No. I'm in conference with myself.

OLO: Why are you so eager to get hold of a radio today?

BODZIO: Because I have a right to it… I can't bear listening to my own voice or yours any longer.

OLO: Have a nap then.

BODZIO: Don't you know by now, my little spastic, that I only sleep four hours a day? Sleep yourself, bloody pipsqueak. Maybe you'll dream about your famous daddy… Publishing a book every year. Travelling abroad. Translated into every language in the world.

OLO: I never said his books were translated into every language in the world. Do you know, grandpa, how many languages there are in the world?

BODZIO: Well, how many?

OLO: Over two thousand.

BODZIO: Fing-pang-ping.

OLO: What?

BODZIO: I was speaking Chinese… But your old man might send you a bit of money, if they publish his books all over the place. All over the world.

OLO: He's only been translated into the most important languages. English, Russian, French, Italian, Spanish, German …

BODZIO: Esperanto, Cretinanto, Elephanto …

OLO: Too much for your little brain to take in, eh? Too hard. And you're envious too.

BODZIO: If he were a joiner and he'd won the lottery I'd envy him… But even then I don't know… What could I do with the money now?

OLO: True. I wouldn't know what to do with it either.

BODZIO: I was talking about big money. Small amounts always come in handy… You could buy papers, whichever you liked, and some of your beloved books, and get some decent grub delivered from town… You'd feel better… You could always slip a nurse a few coppers and get better treatment.

OLO: It's not too bad now.

BODZIO: Idiot! I suppose you're going to tell me you're quite happy with your illness, are you?… You could do with some money.

OLO: I don't want anything from them, grandpa… If they sent me money they'd feel they had the right to come and see me.

BODZIO: And would it bother you if they did?

OLO: Yes, it would.

BODZIO: Why?

OLO: How many times do I have to tell you, you old sclerotic? They'd remind me of the past, and I have to put all that behind me.

BODZIO: And can you?

OLO: No.

BODZIO: There you are then.

OLO: But their visits would be like ripping the bandage off a wound, at one pull… And that hurts. I'd be furious if they turned up, and stay furious after they'd gone. As things are it's easier… I only get mad at you, you old King Herod.

BODZIO: I'll get you some day for that 'King Herod'.

OLO: Go ahead, go ahead.

BODZIO: When they wheel us out onto the terrace I'll strangle you, you cheeky bugger.

OLO: You'll need strong arms for that.

BODZIO: I've still got enough strength in these arms. Tomorrow you'll see.

OLO: Watch out, Bodzio, or I'll throw a glass at you.

BODZIO: You'd do better to take a look in the mirror, Olo. What a mug!

OLO: Are you ringing that bell again?

BODZIO: Aren't I allowed to?

OLO: If she said she'd bring a radio she'll bring one. You can count on Sophie.

BODZIO: She's a slut like all the rest.
OLO: She puts everything she's got into it… Amazing really.
BODZIO: Seen her at it in bed, have you?
OLO: I mean into her work looking after us. It's no fun, and it doesn't even pay well. But have you ever seen her get up-tight? You can always count on her. She puts her back into the dirty work she has to do around us.
BODZIO: Why do you stick up for her like that? You won't get your leg over. How could you?
OLO: Talking to me?
BODZIO: No, to the saints above.
OLO: Take your finger off that bell.

(Door opens)

NURSE: Is it about the radio or the bed-pan?
BODZIO: My beautiful angel, we'd like the radio.
NURSE: I'll bring it in a moment. I meant to earlier …

(Door closes)

OLO: Run off her feet.
BODZIO: Some women like hard work… They're too stupid to take it easy.
OLO: You're a nasty piece of work, Bodzio.
BODZIO: Idiot! If I tell you lots of women don't feel well when they haven't got work to do, you can take it from me it's true. I've seen a few things in my time. They have to keep on dusting even though everything's gleaming, – washing windows, polishing floors… My old lady was like that, God rest her soul… Always finding work to do… You got a big flat?
OLO: I've told you a thousand times. I live in a villa.
BODZIO: Oh yes, so you said.
OLO: I'm only sorry about the pictures.
BODZIO: Why's that? What do you care about them?
OLO: I'd got used to them… I was fond of some of them… The two pictures from my room would go nicely here.
BODZIO: Isn't that winter scene enough for you?
OLO: That's a photo.
BODZIO: Aren't we fussy? You're as particular as a lord.
OLO: Oh well... Even pictures don't matter much any more. *(Chuckling)* At one time I wanted to study the history of art.
BODZIO: What sort of job do you get after that?
OLO: You get to be an art historian.
BODZIO: And what does that give you?

OLO: You can be a curator in a museum, you can write in the papers about exhibitions, you can do research... There are several possibilities...
BODZIO: And do they pay?
OLO: Not very well...
BODZIO: You're not missing much then.
OLO: Shut it, grandpa.
BODZIO: Who are you talking to?
OLO: Myself.
BODZIO: That's all right then. Does your mum like cleaning and tidying?
OLO: No.
BODZIO: Your villa must be a bit of a tip then.
OLO: The maid does the cleaning and tidying... Except in my father's study. He won't let anybody touch anything in there. He has piles of papers on his desk, but he knows exactly where everything is... It's a nice study... A big, dark desk...
BODZIO: What sort of wood?
OLO: How should I know? I'm not a joiner, like you. A big, dark desk, and a hard chair behind it with a high, carved back. Uncomfortable as hell, but the old man says he works better on it.
BODZIO: That bitch was going to bring the radio straight away...
OLO: Two deep leather-covered armchairs in the corner... Bookshelves all around... Walls lined with books from floor to ceiling.
BODZIO: So where are the pictures? On the ceiling?
OLO: One facing the desk, between two bookcases, and one over the door... Abstract geometry... The one facing the desk's a surrealistic cityscape.
BODZIO: A what?
OLO: A surrealistic cityscape.
BODZIO: You'll get your tongue tied in knots if you're not careful.
OLO: A strange city, all made of marble. Naked women with birds' heads in the streets.
BODZIO: In the picture, you mean?
OLO: Where do you think? Ever seen a bird's head on a naked woman?
BODZIO: Nor on one with her clothes on, come to that. Why couldn't the artist go and paint something decent, like Saint Joseph or something?

(Door opens. Footsteps)

NURSE: Here's the radio.
BODZIO: Nurse, let me kiss your hand.
NURSE: Don't hurry, Bodzio. I'll turn it on myself.
BODZIO: It's starting in a moment...

NURSE: What?
BODZIO: Nothing... Could you turn it on right away?
NURSE: There you are.
BODZIO: I'll do the rest myself. Just in time. Quarter past.
NURSE: Will that be all, gentlemen?
OLO: Yes, thank you.

(Footsteps. Door closes)

BODZIO: Here we go then...
VOICE FROM RADIO: ... lost three nil to Vistula on their home ground. That was the sporting news. *(Pause)* This is Warsaw speaking. We are now broadcasting a request programme.
OLO: Find another station.
BODZIO: Shut up!
VOICE FROM RADIO: Jurek, from Wyszkow, wishes many happy returns to Miss Jasia Malgowska on her eighteenth birthday. Karolina sends all good wishes to Gabriel Marto, of Gdansk, on his twenty-first. And for Miss Stenia Kuzio we have very best wishes from the Wojcik family on her eighteenth birthday. To Mister Alexander Lipski, Olo to his friends, in the nursing home at Zambowice, love and best wishes from his mother and father on his twentieth birthday. For all of you: a trumpet solo.
BODZIO: *(music in the background)* For you, Olo. Love and best wishes.
OLO: *(pause; music in the background)* Bodzio, I haven't got a family. I grew up in an orphanage... You must have sent in that request.
BODZIO: *(music in the background)* You must have a family if they broadcast it.

(Trumpet solo)

NOBODY DANCES LIKE THAT NOW

(Music for a moment, then silence)

MAN: *(Out of breath)* The record's finished… At last…
GIRL: *(Evenly, not out of breath)* Nobody dances like that now.
MAN: *(after a pause, breathing heavily)* You mean like me?
GIRL: Yes… No one dances like that.
MAN: I just felt like doing a bit of a dance… *(His breathing gradually returns to normal).*
GIRL: You put too much energy into it… Jigging and jumping this way and that, a million movements too many. And what a pace you set!
MAN: I was following the beat.
GIRL: Yes, but there's no need for all that… These days it's different, no hurry… Like me… I was following the beat too.
MAN: I'm tired out.
GIRL: You could have danced the way I did.
MAN: I'm not sure I know how to.
GIRL: Nothing to it… Anyway, your way's harder, almost acrobatic.
MAN: That used to be the style..
GIRL: When?
MAN: A few years back… Seventeen years ago, to be exact.
GIRL: I was three then..
MAN: I haven't danced since then… Till today.
GIRL: I thought we'd come here for something else.
MAN: I suddenly felt like dancing.
GIRL: You take dancing too seriously. Ought to relax more. You dance as if your life depended on it.
MAN: *(with an embarrassed titter)* Do I really?
GIRL: Wipe your forehead. You're perspiring.
MAN: I'm tired out.
GIRL: You could have danced the way I did.

(Brief pause)

MAN: Would you like something to drink?
GIRL: No, I'd like an apple.

MAN: Right.

(He goes out. Music starts again, softer now. Man's footsteps)

GIRL: I don't need a knife. I prefer apples with the peel. What have you got in that glass?
MAN: Vodka and tonic. Turn the record-player off.
GIRL: That's a good record.
MAN: I don't like it any more. Turn it off.

(Silence. Crunch of Girl's teeth on apple)

GIRL: *(chewing)* Not a bad system. A stereo like that sets you back a bit, eh?
MAN: You can have the record.
GIRL: Do you mean it?
MAN: The sleeve for it's over there.
GIRL: Thanks…

(Crunch of teeth on apple)

MAN: Put it in the sleeve, so you don't forget it.
GIRL: I'm not leaving yet… Unless you want me to.
MAN: I don't want to see that record any more.
GIRL: You're funny…
MAN: Because nobody dances like that now.
GIRL: Of course they don't. There, I've put it away. Happy now?
MAN: Yes… You've got nice breasts.
GIRL: Let me finish my apple first.
MAN: No apple can compare…
GIRL: … and then I'll undress.
MAN: There's no hurry.
GIRL: That's good. I like just sitting like this… It's not really light any more, and it's not really dark either… How much did you pay for that stereo?
MAN: I brought it back from Holland. The converted price doesn't mean much.
GIRL: It's nice here…*(Crunch of apple being chewed)* This armchair's so comfortable… *(Pause)* Say something.
MAN: Why.
GIRL: I don't know… So's to say something.
MAN: Does it matter that much to you?
GIRL: No, but it's nice to hear somebody talking. Heads down! Fire!
MAN: Throwing apple cores is a serious art. Not everybody can do it.
GIRL: It missed your head by a centimetre.
MAN: Your health.

GIRL: Does it taste good?
MAN: Not bad.
GIRL: I can't bear vodka… Where do I go for a pee?
MAN: First door on the left in the hall.
GIRL: Have fun while I'm away.

(Exit. Man sighs deeply, then his steps are heard. Music starts again, the same as before, very soft. Girl's footsteps returning)

GIRL: That record really grabs you, doesn't it?
MAN: I just wanted to hear it again.
GIRL: I'll give it back if you like.
MAN: Don't be silly. (*Turns off record-player*)
GIRL: Wife away, is she?
MAN: I'm not married.
GIRL: Then whose are those cosmetics in the medicine cabinet?
MAN: Somebody left them.
GIRL: She must have had plenty of money. They're expensive things. I wouldn't have left them.
MAN: They're nearly empty.
GIRL: Nearly empty? They're hardly started.
MAN: You can take them… But you don't need any cosmetics… You can manage without them for a few years yet.
GIRL: That's what you think.
MAN: They're yours if you want them.
GIRL: Thanks. You're so generous.
MAN: Your health.
GIRL: It's disgusting the way you drink. So greedily.
MAN: Another apple?
GIRL: No… *(Pause)* Some day I'll have a flat like this. Maybe even better.
MAN: I'm sure you will.
GIRL: You don't have to believe me, but if I say I will, I will.
MAN: When you get your degree and go out to work, of course you will.
GIRL: You don't believe me. You're grinning over your glass. Finish your drink!
MAN: Don't rush me, sweetie.
GIRL: You have to work for years to get a place like this… but I'll do it faster… I'll get married, or…
MAN: Win the pools.
GIRL: Pity you didn't give me another apple. I'd have thrown it at you, and hit you. Right between the eyes.
MAN: Do you think you'd be happy if you had a nice flat?
GIRL: Of course I would.

MAN: That's what you say now, but when you eventually get your dream flat you won't be so sure.
GIRL: What do you know about it? I share two rooms with four others.
MAN: With a kitchen?
GIRL: Yes.
MAN: Ye-e-es…
GIRL: There's my parents, my sister, my brother and me… My brother sleeps in the kitchen.
MAN: How old is he?
GIRL: What's it to you?
MAN: Nothing.
GIRL: Fifteen.
MAN: So you and your sister share the other room?
GIRL: Yes.
MAN: Don't look so sulky.
GIRL: I'm not.
MAN: Sure you don't want a drink?
GIRL: I've told you: I can't stand alcohol.
MAN: Most girls of your age…
GIRL: My father drinks, and that's enough for me.
MAN: What are you studying?
GIRL: Maths… What were you doing at the university?
MAN: I went there to see a friend.
GIRL: Or did you go on the pick-up?
MAN: No, I went to see a friend.
GIRL: And you picked me up.
MAN: You had a nice, dreamy look… You were smiling to yourself.
GIRL: Soft soap.
MAN: Want to go out for supper afterwards?
GIRL: Was it really because I had a nice dreamy look?
MAN: That and a few other things.
GIRL: At least you're honest… No, I don't want to go out for supper. I'd rather sit here… Haven't you got anything to eat in the house?
MAN: There's some food in the fridge.
GIRL: Then I'll make you some supper.
MAN: If you like.
GIRL: You don't sound too ecstatic about it.
MAN: Don't I really?
GIRL: I know what I'm talking about.
MAN: Sometimes there's an alarming discrepancy between one's ideas and reality. I though girls liked going to a good restaurant…
GIRL: … after a bit of fun in bed.
MAN: That's what I thought.

GIRL: Well I'd rather sit quietly... *(laughing)* Or lie quietly.
MAN: What's your name?
GIRL: Nothing unusual. Maria. Everybody calls me Majka. What's yours?
MAN: Henryk. Everybody calls me Henio.
GIRL: Don't tease.
MAN: *(after a pause)* I ought to get a dog.
GIRL: What for?
MAN: It'd lie in my lap... I'd stroke it... This is just the time for stroking a dog.
GIRL: It'd have to be a little dog. A dachshund, or something about that size. Otherwise it wouldn't fit on your lap.
MAN: If it was bigger it could lie on the settee. I'd sit beside it.
GIRL: Are you trying to tell me you're lonely?
MAN: No. I mean I could do with a dog.
GIRL: You've got me.
MAN: Oh, you are a silly girl.
GIRL: That's not what my professor thinks.
MAN: What year are you in?
GIRL: Second year... Tell me, what exactly do you do?
MAN: You mean my job?
GIRL: Yes.
MAN: Dancing too fast... Jigging and jumping this way and that, a million movements too many. *(Girl laughs)*
GIRL. *(gently)* You don't have to tell me if you don't want to.
MAN: Shall I put another record on?
GIRL: I'd rather sit here and not listen to any music.
MAN: Do you think you'll be happy when you have a nice flat, a car, furniture and a lot of household gadgets and things?
GIRL: That's what I think now, because I haven't got any of them.
MAN: I envy you your faith.
GIRL: Are you trying to tell me you're unhappy?
MAN: Oh, it's not that simple.
GIRL: Buy yourself a dog... Or if we still know each other tomorrow, I'll bring you one from the pound. You haven't anything against mongrels, have you?
MAN: No.
GIRL: Who'll look after it? Will you have time for a dog?
MAN: No.
GIRL: There you are then. But there's no harm in day-dreaming. It's good for you... Drink up that vodka, will you?
MAN: It's more tonic than vodka... Besides, I wouldn't know what to do with my hands.

GIRL: I thought you liked me.
MAN: I do. Very much.
GIRL: But you don't want a re-run of the same old routine, is that it?
MAN: Yes I do… In a minute.
GIRL: Soft soap.
MAN: Have you got a boyfriend?
GIRL: What's it to you?
MAN: Nothing.
GIRL: No. Just now and again.
MAN: It's nearly dark.
GIRL: I know what you were thinking about just now… The other day I had a dream that I was giving some very important paper at a conference somewhere abroad. There were lots of top scientists there. My paper was applauded, and then I started back to my hotel, all alone in a strange city and I lost my way. I was in despair… I woke up in tears… But it was only a dream.
MAN: You'll be successful, and you won't go home alone.
GIRL: But that won't change anything. That's what you mean, isn't it?
MAN: No.
GIRL: What did you mean, then?
MAN: You've got aspirations and a warm personality. That's a good innoculation.
GIRL: Against what?
MAN: Against what?… Maybe against discouragement.
GIRL: It's easy for you to talk. You've got everything you ever wanted.
MAN: Everything I ever wanted, you say… This isn't at all what I wanted.
GIRL: Then what did you want?
MAN: I don't remember… Or I don't want to remember…
GIRL: You talk like an old man, and you're not at all old. How old are you?
MAN: Thirty-six.
GIRL: You look more like thirty.
MAN: May Heaven reward you, my child.
GIRL: I only hope I don't have to wait too long… *(Pause)* I like you.
MAN: What's your set-up at home?
GIRL: What do you mean?
MAN: I mean, can you stay the night?
GIRL: Yes… if I want to.
MAN: (*after pause*) I wasn't talking like an old man… Like a young lad would be more like it… I feel younger with you, Marysia.
GIRL: Majka.
MAN: Majka.

GIRL: That's good, because I don't like old men.
MAN: Your health.
GIRL: Drink it all up.

(Silence)

MAN: Happy now?
GIRL: Put that glass down.
MAN: I like to have something to play with.
GIRL: You know what that means?
MAN: I see you haven't only studied maths, but psychology as well.
GIRL: Put it down.
MAN: O tyrant with the lovely breasts.
GIRL: You haven't seen them yet… Put it down… Are you afraid of me?

(Tap of glass on table-top)

GIRL: *(laughing)* You've got aspirations too… It's done something to you.
MAN: You know what? I think that when I was your age I was like you.
GIRL: With certain differences.

(Both laugh)

MAN: I mean it. I was sure of everything… so confident.
GIRL: Don't get sentimental.
MAN: You're right.
GIRL: Who left those cosmetics?
MAN: What does it matter?
GIRL: You're terribly discreet.
MAN: A raven-haired blonde.
GIRL: Aha… and you still feel hung over?
MAN: *(laughing)* Oh no, not a bit… She hopped about even more than me.
GIRL: *(after pause)* She was older than me, wasn't she?
MAN: Yes.
GIRL: You have to do it slowly, effortlessly… taking it easy…
MAN: You think you'll manage it?
GIRL: I don't know… But I think so.
MAN: You'll have a nice flat… Success.
GIRL: Don't talk like that. If you've got everything it's because… because you flogged yourself to death. And now you've forgotten how to relax.
MAN: That's what you think.
GIRL: I'm quite sure.
MAN: You're very dogmatic.

GIRL: I want you to embrace me.
MAN: Sure.
GIRL: We've been talking too much.
MAN: You're right. But you wanted to.
GIRL: I don't want to talk any more. Come here.
MAN: Majka…
GIRL: Yes?
MAN: Let's have another go at dancing first.
GIRL: Oh, you are a one!
MAN: I want to dance the way you do.
GIRL: All right. Up you get.

(The same music as before. Pause in conversation)

GIRL: There you are. You can do it.

(Music)

MAN: Then you'll put the record away.
GIRL: Don't worry, I will. It'll be one of the best records I have.

(Music)

GIRL: Henryk!
MAN: *(out of breath)* What?!… What?!
GIRL: You're doing it again, dancing the same old way! Too many movements! Nobody dances like that now.

THE TERRARIUM

DOCTOR: You're looking splendid today.

SHE: Your tie's twisted, doctor.

DOCTOR: Thank you. Is that better?

SHE: Yes. What was the noise under the window this morning?

DOCTOR: They were repairing the pavement.

SHE: What an awful noise.

DOCTOR: A pneumatic drill and a jackham…

SHE: *(shouting)* That's enough!

DOCTOR: *(after a pause)* A lot of flowers have come for you.

SHE: Give them out to the nurses.

DOCTOR: There are some letters as well.

SHE: I can't read them. I haven't the strength.

DOCTOR: You ought to.

SHE: Why?

DOCTOR: They're from your friends. And the theatre has sent a lot of letters from your admirers… It's good for you to keep in touch with the real world.

SHE: Don't make me laugh. I know exactly what my so-called friends will say, and I haven't the strength to read letters from any teenage girls or fading provincial blooms. I'm an old woman, doctor. In four years I'll be sixty. I've had plenty of letters in my time… Besides, I'd rather think about my bedsores – that's something definite – than about what my friends might be saying about me in excited whispers… Do you know what a stage whisper is?

DOCTOR: Not exactly.

SHE: It's the sort of whisper that carries right across the theatre. How old are you?

DOCTOR: Thirty-four.

SHE: You look younger… Were you looking after me while I was unconscious?

DOCTOR: No, that was my colleague, a specialist in a different field.

SHE: You're a psychiatrist, aren't you?

DOCTOR: Yes.

SHE: And what's your colleague's speciality?

DOCTOR: He's a neurologist.

SHE: I see... And is there any news about... You know who I mean. Last time you promised to find out.

DOCTOR: And I have. He's very well and he's in Zakopane.

SHE: *(softly)* Zakopane... That fits... He's got lots of friends there, I'm sure. *(In normal voice)* You've done what I asked you to do, and now it's my turn. You want to know about that word I kept repeating... Was I delirious?

DOCTOR: No.

SHE: You're very kind, but most people are when they're unconscious.

DOCTOR: Your diction was flawless.

SHE: Terrarium... Does it have any meaning for me? The only word I kept repeating... What roles have you seen me in?

DOCTOR: The first time I saw you I was still a boy. You were playing Phaedra. You were superb. You were superb in all the roles I saw you in, but that first made the deepest...

SHE: Enough said. Thank you... How old were you then?

DOCTOR: Fifteen.

SHE: And you really remember it?

DOCTOR: Yes.

SHE: *(laughing)* Mercurial adolescent dreams... You saw me for the first time as Phaedra and thought I was superb... I can believe that: a big, well-proportioned woman, a well-known actress, still good-looking, the glare of the footlights, and a fifteen-year-old boy in the audience... That's how you first saw me. And I first saw myself – in a scene that's stayed in my mind – as a pale, ugly little girl with nasty, thin little pigtails.

DOCTOR: No, no. Please don't stop. I'll just straighten your pillow.

SHE: Thank you... I stood in front of the mirror. I was alone in the room. And I looked at myself. So that's me, I thought. *(She chuckles)* My discovery of my identity. I expect you went through something like that yourself when you were a boy.

DOCTOR: Yes, I did.

SHE: I didn't like myself at all, and the longer I looked at myself, the uglier, the more mis-shapen and timid I seemed... But I went on staring, I couldn't stop... It was me... Me, and nobody else... Late afternoon, a greenish light in the room – that was because of the lime-tree we had growing by the window – and me alone in the house, gazing into the greenish depths of the mirror. And there in the mirror, beyond my reflection, was a terrarium. I turned round and went up to it. In the glass box, dozing on some pebbles and moss, was a lizard. There was the lizard, and there was me. I must have looked at it for a long time... Where do you come from?

DOCTOR: I was born in Warsaw.

SHE: Where did you spend your childhood?

DOCTOR: Also in Warsaw.

SHE: I spent mine in a little town near the border. I lived in a little wooden house in the suburbs, if that's the right word for a street that ended in a gully by a river… You won't see any little towns like that these days.

DOCTOR: Did you have any brothers or sisters?

SHE: A brother, but he drowned in the river at the end of the gully. He was five or six then, two years younger than me. I don't remember him, except for his awful whistle. In summer he used to sit in the lime-tree for hours, whistling.

DOCTOR: What about the terrarium?

SHE: Oh yes, I keep digressing… The terrarium was my father's. He was a silent man, thin and bald. He worked as a book-keeper in a sugar-refinery. After work he used to sit by the terrarium and stare at the lizard, drinking vodka and taking no notice of my mother or me. On sunny days he carried the terrarium outside, so the lizard could bask in the sun.

DOCTOR: Was he a loving father to you?

SHE: Sometimes, occasionally… He never struck me… Sometimes he sat me on his kneed, smiled, stroked my head then set me down, sighed, and either went off somewhere or looked at the lizard behind the glass. He alone had the right to feed it. He would bring it insects and other nasty little creatures.

DOCTOR: And what was your mother like?

SHE: Religious, hard-working, terrorized by my father. She was afraid of him, although I don't remember him ever raising his voice at her.

DOCTOR: Were you what they call 'a difficult child'?

SHE: No. I was conscientious at school, quiet, even-tempered. To tell the truth, I was very shy. One of the teachers, an old maid who was said to have had a great romance with an Austrian officer, noticed that I liked reading and started choosing books for me to read. And I must say she didn't have your usual stuffy provincial taste. Oh no, the cow-eyed old beanpole. *(Chuckles) Lives of Wayward Ladies* for a girl of fourteen. In those days, the late 'twenties, that was… Well, you understand, don't you? I don't want to make her sound a satanic corruptress though. Some of the books she gave me I would happily have given to my own daughter, if I'd had one then… Do you know? I never saw my father reading anything. Never one book, nor a paper.

DOCTOR: Did the terrarium hold a fascination for you?

SHE: Apart from that afternoon I was telling you about, no. Perhaps that's not very clear. The terrarium was the focal point of our house, rather like the altar in a chapel... Father used to say the lizard was very old. Maybe it was true, I don't know, or maybe there were several lizards. Anyway, there was always a lizard there behind the glass, among the pebbles and moss. I wouldn't call it fascination. I simply lived in the shadow of the terrarium.

DOCTOR: Aren't you tired yet?

SHE: *(chortling)* Just a bit out of breath. It's because I don't get much exercise.

DOCTOR: If you really aren't tired, then do go on... Just a moment, let's check your pulse... *(Silence for a moment)* Yes. a little bit fast, but nothing unusual.

SHE: Would you mind handing me that mirror? Thank you... Heavens! What a sight! But I promised myself I wouldn't use lipstick and I'll keep my word... What was I talking about? Oh yes, I didn't tell you about the end of that terrarium, Father's terrarium... It was the end of June, a sunny day, with insects humming in the grass. Father was at work. Mother had gone to the market. I'd just taken my matriculation exam and felt a different person, because I was flirting with a boy and dreaming about a new life... I had this sudden impulse... I picked the terrarium up and carried it down to the gully. I let the lizard out. It lay still for a while, then scurried into the grass. I smashed the terrarium into tiny pieces. I had released the lizard into the sunshine, and myself into freedom. I threw some things into a suitcase, took a hundred zlotys from the sideboard – it seemed an enormous sum to me – and ran to the station. I took a train to Warsaw. That was in 1934... How awfully long ago! You weren't even born then.

DOCTOR: You talk about 'that' terrarium as if there was some other terrarium. Was there?

SHE: We'll come to that shortly. Do you want to make a career in science?

DOCTOR: *(laughing, slightly taken aback)* Well, we'll see.

SHE: Never be ashamed of being ambitious, my boy. For myself, I'm sick of being a 'superb performer', as they used to say, and I'll be only too happy to figure in your learned papers as a case study.

DOCTOR: If I...

SHE: Your tie's askew again.

DOCTOR: Is that better?

SHE: Perfect. Who buys your ties for you?

DOCTOR: I buy them myself.

SHE: You ought to buy ties in brighter colours... Or does your professional conformism forbid it?

DOCTOR: Tomorrow I'll wear one in the wildest colours.

SHE: Where do you spend your holidays?

DOCTOR: At the seaside, or in the mountains.

SHE: For about fifteen years I've been spending mine by a little lake in a forest. You can only approach the lake from one side. There's a sloping clearing about two hundred yards wide with a half-timbered house in it. The owner's a bit eccentric, but he's nice. I rent a room there – whitewashed, not much furniture, bunches of fragrant herbs hanging on the walls… I usually go there alone. It's quiet, I can bathe and lie in the sun… Two years ago a yellow tent appeared on the edge of the clearing, right under the trees… They were a handsome couple. She had a dark complexion; he had a light, golden tan… I got to know them one day when they came to see Zalewski, the landlord, to buy some sour milk… Then we went swimming together. She wasn't a very strong swimmer and she was afraid to go far from the shore. But he liked swimming out with me, at his steady, relaxed crawl… They were both students. Would you tell Nurse Janka not to be quite so gentle and cautious – it just draws out the pain. I've told her about it but she *will* see me as someone who's been on TV and in magazines, whereas she ought to see an old woman with bedsores, who can't move. She could be a bit brisker.

DOCTOR: I'll tell her.

SHE: Firmly, mind.

DOCTOR: Of course.

SHE: *(chuckling)* She'll blush.

DOCTOR: Is that lake one of the Mazovian Lakes?

SHE: It's not far from Augustow.

DOCTOR: I don't know those parts.

SHE: I'll give you Zalewski's address. You can take a girlfriend there, doctor. But make sure she's not a dull one, because you really will be condemned to each other's company.

DOCTOR: Thank you. I'd like to go there.

SHE: Unfortunately that couple in the yellow tent had nothing but each other… I noticed that their relations were beginning to deteriorate… They argued, and would go off separately into the wood… She was called Lucyna. She had long legs and almond eyes, and his name was Michael… She called him Mike… They were too young to endure each other's exclusive company twenty-four hours a day… one day Lucyna left. Michael would come and sit beside me. We'd talk idly. He wanted to appear very interesting, which led to a few false notes… He was studying geography, in his fourth year… Do you ever have sudden desires, doctor?

DOCTOR: Of course.

SHE: So do I. I won't try to cast a rosy light on things. I don't suffer from that sort of shame any longer. One night when I came out of the water I wanted Mike… I'd been thinking about myself, I'd forgotten about him for a while… That was a mistake… When he became so boyishly ingratiating, then so boyishly sulky and aggressive, I couldn't resist… Zalewski gave me a strange look, but of course he didn't say anything… Mike rolled up his yellow tent and moved into my room… It was a lovely holiday… Would you pass my stewed fruit? My throat's gone dry.

DOCTOR: Here you are.

(Silence for a moment)

SHE: Very tasty. I don't like it too sweet. This is just right.

DOCTOR: At the beginning of our conversation I mentioned a jackhammer, and you reacted rather sharply. Could you perhaps tell me why those words produced such a reaction?

SHE: I had a dream…

(Silence)

DOCTOR: Yes, go on.

SHE: After I'd come round I kept having this dream… I was smashing panes of glass with a hammer… The crash of shattering glass… *(Chuckles)* An ordinary hammer, not a jackhammer… I don't like that word.

DOCTOR: Thank you.

SHE: Are you writing that down?

DOCTOR: Yes, but I'll put my pad away now. Do go on.

SHE: We went on seeing each other in Warsaw. Hold on… Let me think… *(Pause)* Are you in a hurry?

DOCTOR: Not at all.

SHE: Now I remember. I was wondering how it came about that Mike moved in with me, in my flat in Warsaw… That's right, it was hard to get a place in a hall of residence. He stayed one night, another night, and we somehow got used to the idea without thinking about it. As I say, I've overcome any embarrassment about these things. I didn't feel awkward in the situation. Anyway, my friends were very understanding, and were perfectly natural with Mike. He had this marvellous, puppyish ability to adapt. He felt absolutely at ease with me, and in a way I was proud of his ability to behave so naturally.

DOCTOR: Did he drop his studies?

SHE: No, that is, not yet… In fact he didn't drop them later either. He just postponed his M.A. thesis. I think he'll write it now.

DOCTOR: I think so too.

SHE: I took him to parties. I took him everywhere with me. I wanted to give him a bit of polish, as my director says… I had no illusions. I realized that everything would have been quite different if it hadn't been for my name and my position… Of course, I believed he was one of those boys who have a taste for older women, who like the sort of thrill that only an older woman can provide, but I really didn't delude myself that much… Although I didn't often think about it, I was floating along on a cloud – if that doesn't sound too funny. It ought to, coming from a woman as big as Buddha… Floating along on a cloud of tenderness… *(Chuckles)* Melancholy tenderness… I didn't want anybody standing in my way, so when my ex-husband turned up and told me to stop making a fool of myself, I told him to get out.

DOCTOR: Kamil is very anxious to see you. I told him it was up to you.

SHE: I don't want to see him. I had eight years of looking at him, and that's enough.

DOCTOR: I'll pass that on,… but I won't put it quite so harshly.

SHE: You can repeat what I said word for word. If he came here he'd put on his loathsome, cultivated, hypocritical expression and start saying, 'What did I tell you, my dear?' I don't want to see him. Yes, I threw him out that time… But I might tell you, that's not the only visit I've had on that subject. Young Lucyna, from the lake, came too… I received her in my dressing-room at the theatre. I stage-managed the meeting. I kept my make-up girl there and she was doing my hair when the girl came in. She let fly hard enough, but I offered her a seat with the queenly air that the reviewers praise so highly… The poor, wretched little thing became more unsure of herself and embarrassed with every second… How I envied her that simple view of life, that girlish freshness! She burst into tears and ran out.

DOCTOR: Did you tell Michael about that?

SHE: Yes… After some thought… It was a sort of test for me… Michael just shrugged and went out. He was hurrying to see his tailor… I've always liked my men well dressed.

DOCTOR: What was the other terrarium in your life?

SHE: We'll come to that in a moment… Months passed, a year passed, and I began to felt that something had changed, and yet I knew there was nothing different in any concrete sense. I went on with my acting. Mike was as nice as he always was, the maid was solicitous. Everything seemed to be all right. But I couldn't sleep. For the first time in my life I learned what sleeplessness can be. I started taking tranquillizers and sleeping powders.

DOCTOR: What sort?

SHE: Various kinds. Barbiturates. They helped. Just then I had three weeks off. I went to the lake with Mike, who was terribly reluctant to write that M.A. thesis of his. We returned a few days later. I couldn't stand myself. Mike was wonderful, but I was unbearable. When I got back I realized what the cause of it was. I don't know if I came to it by sudden inspiration, or by logical processes, or introspection. Anyway, that doesn't matter. I realized that my flat and everything around me made up a terrarium... And I was an old immobilized lizard, separated from everybody by a sheet of glass... What would you have done in that situation?

DOCTOR: As a professional man, I'd have turned to a colleague for advice.

SHE: But in my place?

DOCTOR: Alcohol?

SHE: Well done! Alcohol and barbiturates.

DOCTOR: A lethal mixture.

SHE: I know... My days became like nightmares... I must have been awful. Before that I never used to drink, so you can imagine how it was. I got worse and worse. Reality became less and less real. But the phantoms were real enough... I wanted to free myself. One evening when I thought I was sober I took Mike by the hand... He's in Zakopane now, isn't he?

DOCTOR: Yes.

SHE: That's good. He's bound to meet lots of friends there... I took Mike's hand and pulled him after me through the window... The last thing I remember is the tinkle of glass... I knew I had to do it. I had to smash the terrarium in order to be released. The lizard from my childhood had been released into the sunshine, and I into old age.

FIRST PRIZE

VOICE FROM THE RADIO: Here are the results of today's draw in the national lottery. Four, nineteen, twenty-eight, thirty-five, thirty-nine, forty-four. I repeat: Four, nineteen, twenty-eight, thirty-five, thirty-nine, forty-four. And now the regional draw… *(The click of a switch. Silence.)*

HE: Did you hear that?

SHE: I'm not deaf, you know, even if my liver is playing up.

HE: It's my number! We've won a million! Look at the ticket!

SHE: No need to shout.

HE: What? What did you say?

SHE: I said you needn't… It doesn't matter.

HE: That's right. Nothing matters now except… I feel fine, fine. No aches. My heart's normal. And they say a lot of winners can't take it. The shock kills them. *(Speaking faster)* Lot of nonsense. Just listen. Perfectly normal rhythm. Maybe just a tiny bit fast, but that's only to be expected. It's not every day that something like this happens. Listen…

SHE: *(after a moment)* It's pounding like a jackhammer. I'll get you some valerian.

HE: I don't need any valerian. That stuff's for cats.

SHE: *(firmly)* I'll get you some valerian.

(Sound of chair being pushed back. Footsteps.)

HE: The voice read out the numbers. I sat down, looked at my ticket, and then I heard the voice: four… I crossed off the four. Then silence. Then the voice came again: nineteen. I crossed off the nineteen. Then a long, long silence. I thought that must be all, and then suddenly: twenty-eight… I didn't want to tell you about the voice. I thought I must be imagining things. And you always make fun of everything. Everything I like you…

SHE: *(to herself)* One, two, three, four, five, six, seven, eight, nine…

HE: I sat there stock still, pen in hand, waiting. The voice didn't let me down. I heard 'twenty-ei…'

SHE: *(to herself)* Fifteen… *(Aloud)* Don't interrupt now or I'll lose count of the drops. *(To herself again)* Sixteen. seventeen, eighteen, nineteen, twenty. Right, there you are. Five drops more than usual. You've earned it.

HE: Earned some valerian! Is that all I've earned?

SHE: Come on, drink up.

HE: Ugh, what a taste! We ought to keep some sort of liqueur in the house. Blackcurrant or something… Look, let's go to a restaurant. We don't need to scrimp and save any longer.

SHE: You haven't got the money yet.

HE: I'll get it next week.

SHE: Oho! The first person singular. You soon get the idea, don't you? I thought *we* were getting it.

HE: You said it yourself: *you* haven't got the money yet.

SHE: I might have been testing you.

HE: Can't you cut out your little games even on a day like this? Let's go to a restaurant. A drop of brandy, salad with a slice of lemon… Pity we've had lunch… You know what? Let's have dinner in a restaurant.

SHE: We'll stay at home. Better to stay at home on a day like this.

HE: *(uncertainly)* Do you think so?

SHE: It's quite obvious.

(A moment's silence.)

HE: A million… Pity it didn't come sooner.

SHE: What do you mean by that?

HE: Twenty years ago or so. It's different when you're young, just over forty. Then…

SHE: I see. Wine and women, is that it?

HE: Marcysia, how could you? Did I ever give…

SHE: Apparently only for want of an opportunity.

HE: Want of an opportunity?

SHE: You said it yourself. If you'd had the money it seems you would…

HE: Do you, with all your experience of the world, seriously think that opportunity… Do you think love affairs and money go together?

SHE: On the whole, yes.

HE: I don't think so.

SHE: What do you mean by that?

HE: The number of times I've asked you to stop saying 'What do you mean by that?'! I might as well be talking to a tree-stump.

SHE: What do you mean by that?

HE: By what?

SHE: You know perfectly well what I mean.

HE: That money isn't everything. Is that what you mean?

SHE: More or less. As usual you're twisting the sense of what you said a moment ago. What opportunities did you have for a bit of excitement?

HE: Anybody with reasonable looks and a bit of charm attracts members of the opposite sex.

SHE: Including you. So that's what you meant.

HE: I didn't say I took advantage of it.

SHE: Oho! And why not?

HE: Because of my duty to my family…

SHE: I thought it was customary to mention love for one's wife as the main reason for rejecting the advances of loose women.

HE: They weren't loose.

SHE: It's not the women I'm interested in at the moment.

HE: I thought…

SHE: Duty. Just duty. When I've kept house these forty years, cooked, cleaned, done your washing…

HE: I beg your pardon, but I've never seen you doing any washing.

SHE: Do you suppose the linen walked by itself to the washerwoman before the war and the laundry after it?

HE: Oh, I know you did that.

SHE: And now, after a life of devotion to you, you tell me that only duty kept you from going wenching.

HE: Stop that! On this Sunday of all Sundays, when Fate has handed us a million, we shouldn't be…

SHE: A moment ago you said it was a voice, not Fate. You said you heard a voice dictating numbers to you.

HE: I'm sure I did.

SHE: A man's voice or a woman's?

HE: Sometimes things happen by telepathy, second sight, and science can't yet explain them. There's nothing funny about it. Anyway, thanks to that voice we've won a million.

SHE: A man's voice or a woman's?

HE: I'm practically certain I heard it.

SHE: So it was a woman's voice.

HE: But even if I imagined that voice…

SHE: Imaginary tarts whispering sweet nothings in your ear.

HE: Lots of people imagine things. There's a special science dealing with it. It's called psychotronics. I read about it not long ago.

SHE: I expect it was a voice you knew. You were thinking about one of the office girls from way back. And I'm sure she wasn't reeling off a string of digits.

HE: Not digits, of course not. Only one digit: four. The others were numbers. I've told you the difference often enough between a digit and a number.

SHE: You were imagining some smutty murmurings while doodling aimlessly on the ticket with your pen.

HE: I heard those numbers.

SHE: So you don't deny it was a woman's voice?

HE: Just numbers. Nothing else.

SHE: Heavens, what filth! *(Pause)* Tolek, what's wrong? You've turned so pale.

HE: I don't know. Maybe it's joy at winning. I've read there've been cases where people have actually died…

SHE: Don't talk about death. You'll outlive me by at least twenty years.

HE: *(sullenly)* I don't want to live longer than you. You'd only hold it against me. (*Sharply*) Even on the day I win a million you can't refrain from your…

SHE: All is clear. For the second time you've emphasized the fact that *you've* won it.

HE: Who else? Who filled in the ticket?

SHE: Who heard the voice?

HE: Well? Who heard it? I heard it.

SHE: I didn't hear any voices, because I'm normal.

HE: And you didn't win.

SHE: I wish you joy of it.

HE: Thank you.

SHE: Go on and enjoy your winnings! Drink them away, wench them away…

HE: Too late for that now.

SHE: Really?

HE: I won it. My name's on the ticket. Nobody else's.

SHE: I won't stand in your way.

HE: I don't say I want to get all the benefit myself, only that I won it… I don't mind if we both, together… All I ask is that you change your ways.

SHE: What? Have I at the age of sixty-three got to sell myself for money.

HE: If you don't want to be nicer you don't have to.

SHE: Now wait a minute. You don't get out of it that easily. What about shared property in marriage?

HE: What do you mean by that?

SHE: Aha, I see you've picked it up.

HE: What do you mean by that?

SHE: Half a million to me, according to the law.

HE: Peace and quiet's worth half a million! *(Bringing fist down on table)* I can afford it!

SHE: Hurt you hand?

HE: For half a million I can afford not to answer that.

SHE: Tolek, you look so pale… Give me your hand.
HE: There's nothing wrong with it. I've got strong hands.
SHE: I want to check your pulse. You're as white as a sheet.
HE: There's nothing wrong with me.
SHE: Don't be so stubborn. Give me your hand. You look as if…
HE: As a matter of fact I don't feel too…
SHE: Give me your hand. There there, good boy, good boy… *(Silence)* Oh, Lord! Your pulse is going wild… Sit still, stay here.

(Hurried footsteps, the sound of dialling on a telephone)

SHE: Ambulance? Could you come at once to Happy Lovers' Street, number seven, flat three? The name's Makowski. Ground floor. A man… Sixty-seven… heart attack… No, I won't let him move. We'll be expecting you. *(Sound of receiver being replaced)* Did you hear? You're not to move.
HE: But I haven't had a heart attack.
SHE: You might have one yet.
HE: But I won't.
SHE: You never know.
HE: They could make us pay a fine for a false alarm.
SHE: You can afford it.
HE: That's not the way I'd choose to spend my winnings.
SHE: Don't worry. You won't have to pay. You've just about got the pulse rate of a corpse.
HE: Your usual accuracy of expression is deserting you.
SHE: What do you expect, when I see my husband looking like a corpse…
HE: I'll have a look in the mirror.
SHE: Sit still. You're not to move.
HE: I haven't had a heart attack.
SHE: Sit still, and keep calm, or you will.

(Silence)

HE: Thank you, Marcysia… You're so good to me.
SHE: I've always been good to you, but you haven't always appreciated it.
HE: Yes I have. My old friends from the office will tell you I've never spoken about you in anything less than superlatives.
SHE: There's nothing to be afraid of. You won't die.
HE: *(uncertainly)* I'm not afraid.
SHE: Superlatives, you say?
HE: Yes. You can take my word for it.

SHE: If you're so anxious to assure me of it, you must be afraid... Death's not so awful, especially death by heart attack. Click, and that's the end of it. I wouldn't mind going out that way... I'm here beside you. You don't have to buy me with nice words.

HE: You've got a nice smile.

SHE: Do you remember how my dentures pinched when I first got them?

HE: Yes.

SHE: Now I don't feel them at all. And my teeth look natural... They haven't got that bluish sheen on them.

HE: Ow! *(Followed by a less clearly articulated groan)*

SHE: What is it? Your heart?

HE: No, that beef I had for dinner. It was a bit tough.

SHE: From now on you'll be dining in restaurants. You'll have the very best of chefs at your beck and call.

HE: You're not to blame if the meat's tough. It's the animal's fault.

SHE: When you dine out, everything tastes better than at home.

HE: Marcysia, your culinary skills are equal to any chef in a top international hotel.

SHE: Now that's going too far! So I'm no more than a cook to you.

HE: Don't misunderstand me.

SHE: I understand you only too well. You never hear *my* voice, do you?

HE: I hear it every day.

SHE: That's not what I mean. A caressing voice right in your ear, dictating numbers and saying smutty things.

HE: I dream about you sometimes.

SHE: I can just imagine how!

HE: Well...

SHE: No, I don't want to hear it.

(Silence)

HE: Do you really want a divorce?

SHE: Of course I do.

HE: After forty years of marriage?

SHE: You've got a short memory... Forty years and nine months, my dear.

HE: The first months together were good.

SHE: Yes, you remember some things. But you never noticed my devotion.

HE: Shame we never had any children.

(Silence)

SHE: Give me your hand... It's a bit slower now... You're as healthy as a bull.

HE: I'll get a driving licence.
SHE: What do you mean by that?
HE: I mean I'll get a driving licence.
SHE: Whatever for?
HE: I'll buy a car and drive about. There are all sorts of nice things to see.
SHE: And plenty of road accidents too.
HE: I'll be careful.
SHE: No good being careful if you're gazing all around you.
HE: I managed all right in the cavalry, and a horse is a living creature, harder to handle than a machine.
SHE: And when was that?
HE: *(after pause)* Oh, a long time ago.
SHE: And you expect me to look after you if you hurt yourself?
HE: If anything happens it'll happen to both of us. We'll go driving together.
SHE: I didn't win my life in a lottery.
HE: You underestimate me as a driver.
SHE: Why should I do anything else?
HE: That's the way you are.
SHE: Have you ever driven a car? Would you even be able to find the hooter?
HE: Men were born to drive.
SHE: What do you need a car for?
HE: To drive about.
SHE: I'd be ashamed at my age to climb into a box and…
HE: I've always wanted a car.
SHE: Too late now.
HE: No it isn't. I've won. I've won half a million and I can do what I like. And you can do what you like with your share.
SHE: So I shall.
HE: A big, black car… I'll drive up to the office…
SHE: Oh no, not the office. There are too many of those ladies there who like fastening their suspenders when there are men looking.
HE: These days they wear tights.
SHE: I wear stockings… Just a moment, my dear. How come you're so familiar with female topography? How do you know what women wear?
HE: From the papers, and the radio, and television.
SHE: Been peeping, have we?
HE: A big, black car… That's the job for me.
SHE: Been peeping, have we?
HE: Nobody can prevent me driving to the office.
SHE: You won't be driving anywhere.

HE: Aren't you getting a divorce, then?

SHE: I said you won't be driving to the office, and that's final.

HE: I'll have to show the car off to somebody.

SHE: You won't be showing off in front of anybody.

HE: The prize has no point if nobody envies you. Let them all see that old Mister M's struck a patch of luck. Let them envy me.

SHE: How are you feeling?

HE: Oh, leave off! I feel fine… What's wrong? Why are you crying?

SHE: *(Snivelling)* It's the way you talk…

HE: I'm talking sense… I'm sorry, Marcysia. Everything'll turn out all right.

(The swelling wail of an ambulance outside the window. Brakes. Silence)

SHE: They're here. I'm glad they've come, because you haven't won a million.

HE: What do you mean by that?

SHE: I didn't post the ticket. I didn't want to waste money on the lottery.

HE: *(Laughing)* You can't fool me like that. What about this control sticker on the ticket?

SHE: For months now I've been using the same sticker and sticking it on every new ticket. *(Weeping)* I steam it off.

HE: *(in a whisper)* You what?

SHE: *(screaming)* I steam it off! I steam it off!

HE: What do you mean by that? *(Softly)* What do you mean…

(Doorbell rings)

THE WINDOW

SHE: Are you going to sit by that window much longer?
HE: I don't know.
SHE: You've been there more than three hours.
HE: Possibly.
SHE: I don't understand how someone like you can…
HE: Shut the door. You're letting the light in.
SHE: Does it dazzle you?
HE: No, I just don't want to be seen. *(Sound of door being closed)* Thank you.
SHE: I don't understand how someone like you can waste time like this.
HE: I'm not wasting time.
SHE: Ouch, dammit!
HE: What is it?
SHE: I bumped my knee on the chair. All because you have to sit in the dark.
HE: You've had time to get used to the arrangement of the furniture.
SHE: Did you have to move that chair?
HE: I suppose I did.
SHE: If you were some old gaffer in a village I wouldn't be so surprised at you. I've seen plenty of old men sitting at the window, gazing out into the street. But you…
HE: What about me?
SHE: You're only thirty-three.
HE: I'm *already* thirty-three.
SHE: Less of your cleverness… This has been going on for six days. As soon as you get home from work you sit down at the window and stare. You sit in the dark and stare. Even at night you come into this room and sit by the window. Do you think I sleep as soundly as all that? I don't. Last night and the night before I woke up, and you weren't in bed.
HE: Well, what of it?
SHE: It's just not like you. You were never like this before. I've known you for two years. You were always so active. I've always felt secure with you.

HE: Don't you feel secure now?

SHE: Oh, yes... but now everything's different. You won't relax. You used to relax by reading, sleeping, thinking about things, or sometimes talking to me. Now you don't even seem to think while you stare out of that bloody window... You're like a block of wood, or stone, or...

HE: Or a lifeless body, eh?

SHE: Stop it, Robert. I'm worried about you.

HE: For pity's sake! Can't I do what I like?

SHE: Yes, but...

HE: But what?

SHE: I'm worried about you.

HE: Look to yourself. You've got heaps of friends, you've got your job, the TV, your tender heart and a well equipped kitchen. You can do three hundred and thirty-three things in one day. But leave me in peace!

SHE: Yes, of course. But I love you.

HE: That's fine then...

(Silence for a moment)

SHE: You haven't even touched me for a week.

HE: You said yourself, we've been together for two years. An interval like that is perfectly normal.

SHE: You know that's not what I mean. You literally haven't touched me. You haven't caressed me, or taken my hand, or kissed me good-night, nothing. I don't seem to exist for you these seven days. All that matters is the window. I can't understand... There's nothing happening in the street. Occasionally somebody passes by, and that's all. There isn't even any traffic to look at.

HE: I'm not looking at the street... You're right. Nothing interesting happens in the street.

SHE: You're not looking at the street?

HE: No.

SHE: So I was right. You're just staring into space, just wool-gathering.

HE: *(in a tired voice)* Why must you sound so triumphant about it?

SHE: Daydreaming! Staring and not seeing anything... Robert, you must realize there's no point in it... Let's go out dancing tonight.

HE: Go with somebody else.

SHE: You don't care about me.

HE: I said you can go with somebody else. That's all.

SHE: If you cared about me you wouldn't say that.

HE: I prefer looking at that window to dancing. That's all.

SHE: That window? Which window?

HE: The third from the left, on the fourth floor of the building opposite.

SHE: It's dark. What can you expect to see in a darkened window?
HE: It's always been dark.
SHE: So?
HE: Seven days ago I saw…
SHE: A woman?
HE: No, not a woman. A match. Somebody struck a match. It flared for a moment, then went out.
SHE: So what?
HE: Nothing. That's all.
SHE: Is that why you've been sitting at the window all this time? Do you expect me to believe anything as stupid as that? Tell me the truth, Robert. You must have something on your mind.
HE: There's nothing on my mind.
SHE: Then why do you sit here?
HE: I want to see that little flame again, in that room that's always dark. *(The woman laughs)* When I see it again I'll stop sitting in the kitchen and we'll go out dancing, or…
SHE: *(softly)* A little flame… *(She laughs slightly hysterically)*
HE: Yes. A little flame in the darkness… Don't you like watching TV in a dark room?
SHE: That's quite different. You see something happening on the screen. Surely you're not going to say a burning match is like a good film?
HE: But I am. A flame can mean more than a film. And be more interesting.
SHE: Would you tell your friends in the factory that?
HE: I don't know… Maybe… But they wouldn't insist on knowing why I sit by the window.
SHE: But I have some right to…
HE: Yes, and I've told you what you wanted to know. So now leave me alone.
SHE: Just a moment, Robert… When I came in you told me to shut the door, because you didn't want anybody to see you in the light. Who did you think might see you?
HE: *(growing agitated)* I've got a feeling there's somebody sitting by the window in that room, staring at our window. I'd rather he didn't see me.
SHE: Why not?
HE: I don't know… But I'd rather he didn't.
SHE: Is all this really the truth?
HE: Why should I tell you lies?
SHE: It just sounds so odd.
HE: For pity's sake! People do odder things than this. Some people stand on their hands for hours and that's supposed to be admirable

because it's yoga and good for the health. Others get drunk every day and nobody seems to mind. Others spend all day sitting on steps gazing straight in front of them. Lots of people do what you call 'odd' things.

SHE: You can't wriggle out of it like that, Robert. People do yoga because they believe in it, and get drunk because they're alcoholics, and sit around in frayed pants because they're suckers for fashion… But you have no *reason* to behave like this… *(Louder)* I know you inside out, and you've no reason.

HE: *(calmly)* Why the hell do I need a reason?

SHE: Nobody does anything without a reason.

HE: That home-spun psychology of yours is… Oh, never mind… Of course there's a reason. I want to see another match burning there.

SHE: What if nobody ever strikes another match there?

HE: I won't sit by the window all my life.

SHE: Then you might as well stop right away.

HE: No, because I'm still hoping.

SHE: You think you'll see the flame again?

HE: Yes.

(A moment of silence)

SHE: Wouldn't it be simpler if you went across to that building and the flat with the window…

HE: Look, I think there's somebody in the window now.

SHE: You're imagining things. I don't see anything. Just a reflection on the window-pane. You know I've got good eyesight.

HE: I'm quite sure there was somebody standing there for a moment.

SHE: Maybe somebody was. So wouldn't it be simpler if you went to meet them. Go in and say you're looking for a Mister Green. Then you'll see who lives there, and the place will lose its fascination.

HE: I don't care who lives there.

SHE: Then what in God's name do you care about?

HE: *(calmly)* I've told you already. I want to see a match flaring again behind that darkened window.

SHE: Doesn't that seem at all odd to you?

HE: No.

SHE: Think about it. Try to think about it objectively. An engineer, in his thirties, outgoing, sober…

HE: What?

SHE: *(louder)* A normal person! No eccentricities. And suddenly he drops everything to sit by a …

HE: You're trying to tell me I've lost my marbles. Is that it?

SHE: No, but you must admit…

HE: In that case I have. Be thankful that it takes such a mild form. I might bite people or have delusions, I might…

SHE: Stop it! *(A pause, then a low laugh)* Do you remember how we met?

HE: More or less.

SHE: I remember perfectly. At that party at Stefan's. You were saying such funny things. Then we went out together and that drunk buttonholed us, insisting he'd lost a leg, although he had two legs.

HE: You could phone Stefan now.

SHE: Yes, if you came with me.

HE: No, I'll stay here.

SHE: Then I won't phone him.

HE: As you like.

SHE: Are you bored with me?

HE: No.

SHE: Are you sure?

HE: I said no.

SHE: Then why can't you devote a little of your time to me? Why haven't you noticed me for the past week? Can a burning match really matter more than anything else? More than my body, more than our past? You haven't even noticed that I've bought a new lamp.

HE: Yes I have.

SHE: You didn't say anything.

HE: Why should I say anything? You've bought it and there it is.

SHE: Do you like it?

HE: Yes, it's pretty.

SHE: Do you think a white shade might be better.

HE: White? Perhaps, but that greenish one's all right.

SHE: Only a little while ago you took an interest in the house.

HE: I still do.

SHE: Don't tell lies!

HE: Do I have to be delighted with every new thing, like a child with a new toy? We're only talking about practical household articles.

SHE: That's not so. They make our home.

HE: I don't see it quite like that…

SHE: I thought our home mattered to you, that it was a place you loved, your place. And now I see you might as well be living in a hotel.

HE: Must you be so aggressive about it?

SHE: I don't mean to be aggressive.

HE: Then try not to be.

SHE: Haven't you ever suffered?

HE: What you're complaining of now hasn't much to do with suffering. As I see it, it's more a case of bad nerves because of a new situation. I once saw a film about some furry animals in a cage that were trained to react to certain signals in a certain order, and when the order of signals was changed the animals became terribly upset.

SHE: *(louder)* You're right. I was used to certain signals, to your touch, to your voice, to the ritual of our love-making, to our daily routine... And now I see that it was all a front, with nothing behind it.

HE: But there is something behind it, my dear.

SHE: *(hysterically)* There isn't!

HE: Yes there is.

SHE: There isn't! There's nothing. It's all fallen down, like a child's set of blocks.

HE: Make yourself some coffee.

SHE: I don't want any coffee.

HE: Have a glass of vodka then. It'll do you good.

SHE: If only it was a woman! If only it was something serious, then at least I'd know that... But to realize you're all alone, and that everything you believed in is an illusion, and all because of a stupid match...

HE: Are you deliberately looking for an argument?

SHE: It's impossible to argue with you... At the moment you're like a lump of wood... Of course I'd like an argument. At least that would be something with some life in it.

HE: Then start one.

SHE: Don't make fun of me.

HE: *(wearily)* Go for a walk, dear. Go wherever you like, but leave me in peace.

SHE: Oh yes, I can go where I like, sleep with whomever I like, and you won't mind a bit... Robert, what's happened?

HE: Nothing. It's just that you won't let me sit by the window... You're the one who's odd.

SHE: I'm like everybody else. I'm normal. Most people are like me. Most of society. They work, have fun, love each other, and people like you want to prevent them doing those things and show them nothing matters.

HE: Look, this room isn't Speakers' Corner.

SHE: Once upon a time your sort used to be put to death.

HE: What sort?

SHE: People who made a show of being different and stood in the way of normal life.

HE: I never used to understand why the women in those old newsreels howled with delight while Hitler was speaking. Now I'm beginning to see...

SHE: I hate you!

HE: And in the Middle Ages women used to egg on the torturer to go at the victims harder with the pincers.
SHE: I hate you!
HE: Because you love me?
SHE: Because I love you as you used to be.
HE: There's some logic in that.
SHE: If I were stronger I'd kill you... Stop staring at that blasted window this minute! Stop it!
HE: Don't tug at me!
SHE: You see if I don't stop you! I'll tell all your friends. I'll make a laughing stock of you! I'll go to a psychiatrist and you'll have treatment, because you're a maniac! A maniac!
HE: All right, but don't tug at me. This is my new jacket.
SHE: I won't let you...
HE: *(shouting)* Careful! *(A pause, then in an even voice)* You see? See the flame? I knew I'd see it again.

(A moment of silence)

SHE: *(gently, in a low voice)* It's gone out.

(The sound of chairs being pushed back.)

HE: I knew I'd see it... Put the light on.

(The click of a switch.)

SHE: Robert...
HE: Yes?
SHE: Robert, I...
HE: Would you like to go out somewhere dancing?
SHE: *(weeping)* I despise myself. I really do.
HE: Are we going to go out dancing or aren't we? I could do with a bit of exercise after all that sitting.
SHE: *(weeping, but less despairingly)* You're not angry?
HE: No.
SHE: If I...
HE: Go to the bathroom, wash your face, do what you can with it, then get changed and we'll go out dancing... Or we'll listen to a bit of music and have a glass of something.
SHE: *(softly, no longer crying)* Robert, I'm sorry about all that... But I was looking at that window and I saw something awful.

THE KIDNAPPING

(A cuckoo clock cuckoos)

HUSBAND: It can't be!

WIFE: Yes it can. It's half past seven. That clock keeps perfect time. My watch says half past seven as well.

HUSBAND: What did you say?

WIFE: You never listen to me. *(Raising voice)* I said it's half past seven.

HUSBAND: So what?

WIFE: You said it couldn't be.

HUSBAND: I didn't mean that… I've just read… No, it can't be.

WIFE: Put that paper down and tell me what you do mean.

HUSBAND: Listen to this: 'UPI reports that one-hundred-and-seven-year-old John Grisson from Utah made a bet that he could eat fifty hard-boiled eggs at one sitting and won his bet. The record-holder feels fine.'

(Pause)

WIFE: If anybody were to overhear us…

HUSBAND: What do you mean?

WIFE: *(bitterly)* Don't you see? Two apparently intelligent people, a professor of engineering and a doctor, conversing like idiots.

HUSBAND: I don't think that at all. It's evening. We're relaxing. I'm reading the paper, you're talking about your watch. What's wrong with that? It's normal.

WIFE: *(after pause)* Yes, it's normal.

HUSBAND: If you're bored, turn on the TV. Even the news is better than an argument.

WIFE: I don't want an argument. *(More softly)* We haven't argued for a long time.

HUSBAND: And you hold that against me.

WIFE: Oh, don't pretend that…

(Footsteps. Sudden loud burst of speech from TV newsreader, then the sound is lower to normal volume. TV news heard for c. 15 seconds. The telephone rings.)

HUSBAND: Hallo, hallo. I can't hear anything. Just a moment. *(To Wife)* Turn it down, will you? *(Silence)* Yes, yes, Godycki speaking.
MALE VOICE *(over telephone)*: Don't interrupt or I'll hang up. I have your son here. He's in a safe place. He's a bit scared, but nothing has happened to him. If you call the police you won't see him alive. That's all for now. We'll discuss the price another time. I don't suppose you'll grudge a few bob for your son, eh?

(Click of disconnection)

WIFE: What is it? Why are you holding the phone like an incense lamp?

(Click of receiver being replaced)

HUSBAND: *(calmly, softly)* Stan's been kidnapped.
WIFE: What?
HUSBAND: Some thugs have kidnapped Stan. One of them said he'd call later about the ransom.

(Silence)

WIFE: *(sharply, hysterically)* Turn it off! I can't bear to watch them opening their mouths when I can't hear anything.
HUSBAND: Easy now, Sophie. Easy… There. It's off.
WIFE: That's better… How much do they want?
HUSBAND: He didn't say. We have to wait for them to call.
WIFE: Did he make any threats?
HUSBAND: If I tell the police…
WIFE: What can we do?
HUSBAND: I think we should tell the police.
WIFE: And lose him? He's my son! I don't agree. We must wait.
HUSBAND: The call might just have been from a private number, not a phone booth. If the police tapped our line they could easily trace it… Even if they phone from a call box I could keep them talking and…
WIFE: *(with anger and pity)* Your precise, analytical mind! *(In normal voice)* Even I realize they can't be as naive as that. They've seen kidnapping films too.
HUSBAND: Do you know where Stan went? To see a friend? To the cinema? Was he meeting a girl?
WIFE: *(subdued)* He said 'Bye' and went out.
HUSBAND: It wouldn't have helped much anyway. They must have picked him up in the street.
WIFE: Stop it! You talk as if it was somebody we didn't even know.
HUSBAND: Getting desperate won't get us anywhere.

WIFE: I know. I'm sorry. *(With sudden aggression)* If you hadn't bought yourself a luxury car nobody would have paid any attention to us.
HUSBAND: And if we hadn't built the house you'd been longing for…
WIFE: *(after pause)* We'll sell the car if we have to.
HUSBAND: We'll see.
WIFE: Does that car matter more to you than your son? Will you miss the old crate that much?
HUSBAND: Don't get me wrong. You can't tell in advance. That's all I meant to say.
WIFE: Give me a glass of brandy.

(Footsteps. Clink of glasses in sideboard.)

HUSBAND: Here you are.
WIFE: Aren't you having any?
HUSBAND: No. I want to be absolutely sober.
WIFE: As usual.
HUSBAND: Even at a time like this you have to…
WIFE: All right, all right… *(drinks)*

(Silence)

HUSBAND: I wonder who they could be. That voice was young and fairly educated, without any regional accent. Although these days, thanks to television, accents are dying out so fast…
WIFE: Shut up!
HUSBAND: *(calmly)* I know I annoy you. But it'll be better if we talk than if we sit here without saying a word.
WIFE: Yes, now you want to talk. But for all those years all you could ever utter was monosyllables.
HUSBAND: You too, Sophie.
WIFE: *(softly)* Why did it have to be like that?
HUSBAND: It didn't have to. It just happened.
WIFE: Remember how I told you I was pregnant?
HUSBAND: We whispered about it all night long.
WIFE: I was sure it'd be a boy.
HUSBAND: And right away we decided we'd call him Stan.
WIFE: Tell me they won't do anything to him. Tell me they won't.
HUSBAND: Everything'll be fine, you'll see.
WIFE: It's only been a few minutes since that damned phone call, but it feels like a year.
HUSBAND: Just as well we didn't get rid of that cuckoo clock… It doesn't go with the furniture, but I like it… It was the first thing we bought – we were so poor then…

WIFE: We bought it even before Stan was born.
HUSBAND: It seemed like madness, but we bought it anyway.
WIFE: Remember a few years ago, when we had this furniture made? I wanted to put the clock in the kitchen but you said we should leave it in the living room. And I agreed at once because I knew what you were thinking... *(Pause)* But I didn't tell you.
HUSBAND: Yes, I remember... I wonder who those people are. Don't look at me like that. We shouldn't be afraid to talk about it. The past won't save us from the present... It'd be best if they believed nobody was involved except us and them. Because like you they've seen films and they know the weak point in a kidnapping is the handover... They can't be panicked.
WIFE: Give me some more brandy.
HUSBAND: Wouldn't it be better if you took something to calm you down?
WIFE: I'm the doctor here and I know what's best for me.

(Footsteps, clinking sounds in sideboard)

HUSBAND: Here you are.
WIFE: Thank you. Mickey... It's a long time since I called you that.
HUSBAND: You're right there.
WIFE: This is good brandy... Tomorrow we'll pick up our savings. Maybe we'll have enough, so you won't need to sell the car.
HUSBAND: Trying to be big-hearted, are we?
WIFE: Don't go spoiling everything.

(Silence)

HUSBAND: The boy isn't sixteen yet.
WIFE: *(on the verge of tears, in muted voice)* It must be dreadful for him.
HUSBAND: They said he was all right, just a bit scared. *(Pause)* And that they're treating him well.
WIFE: *(mimicking him/ contemptuously)* Treating him well!
HUSBAND: You must realize that for the moment he's safe. Those people – if you can call them people – have no interest in harming the boy.
WIFE: I'd like to think you were right.
HUSBAND: Has he had a steady girlfriend?
WIFE: What do you mean by that?
HUSBAND: Any long-term relationship.
WIFE: Oh, you and your eternal trips abroad! You want to know if he's sleeping with anybody, do you?

HUSBAND: More or less. He's well-developed, with a good physique. These days they start early.

WIFE: I don't think he has... Some girls come visiting, but I don't go looking into his room... He goes visiting some girls too, but I don't think there's any more to it. He's still a child. He has sport, and school, and he's never given us any trouble.

HUSBAND: And he's quiet. A typical little introvert.

WIFE: *(after pause)* Why did you ask if Stan had a girlfriend?

HUSBAND: No reason really... I just thought we hardly know anything about him. He's nice, polite and quiet... We only know the exterior.

WIFE: You ought to be at home a bit more often.

HUSBAND: Cut it out.

Wife: If you were you'd know more about him.

HUSBAND: Don't be unfair.

WIFE: Unfair? Me?

HUSBAND: Yes, you. You know how busy I am.

WIFE: Because you're forging your splendid meteoric career.

HUSBAND: *(raising his voice for the first time)* It's not a matter of forging a career! To me my work is... *(more calmly)* Oh, what's the point of telling you?

WIFE: *(insistently)* Go on. I'd like to hear.

HUSBAND: All right, if you like. The fact that you're a doctor defines your professional life, nothing else. I'm not saying you do it badly. I hear you're conscientious, pretty capable and hard-working. But for me science is the most important thing in my life.

WIFE: Of course, because it gives you conferences, grants, honours, money, power, foreign travel and so on.

HUSBAND: All that came later. That's the result. At first it was just hard work... *(Pause)* And it still is hard work. But so absorbing.

WIFE: *(with hysterical laugh)* His son's been kidnapped and he says the most important thing in his life is science! You're a cold fish. You've no heart.

HUSBAND: Don't get carried away by your emotions, Sophie. You know I love him. And you know he occupies less space in my life than my work. But that doesn't mean I don't love the boy.

WIFE: And your home? Does that mean anything to you?

HUSBAND: I haven't had a home for a long time.

WIFE: Really?

HUSBAND: To me a home isn't just a building. It's a family as well. And I have only my son.

WIFE: So I'm dead, am I?

HUSBAND: That's putting it too strongly. You've become distant... You've preferred those strange men – sometimes boys, I hear – whom you visit between five and seven in the evening.

(Silence)

WIFE: So you knew... Why didn't you say so?
HUSBAND: It wouldn't have done any good. And I didn't want to deprive the boy of something that might be called family life.
WIFE: You're a cold, lousy swine.
HUSBAND: Calling me names won't solve anything... Anyway, these last weeks I've been seriously considering divorce. I've come to the conclusion that Stan's big enough and aware enough of certain things to be able to understand me.
WIFE: Aware enough?

(Telephone rings)

HUSBAND: Don't get up. I'll go. Hallo. Godycki here.
MALE VOICE *(on phone)*: We've made a tape-recording of your son, in case you thought he might have come to some harm.

(Pause)

STAN *(on tape)*: Please don't call the police. I feel fine. If you tell the police they'll... Goodbye, see you...

(Click of disconnection)

HUSBAND: It was them. With Stan's voice on tape. He asked us not to call the police and said he feels fine.
WIFE: Give me some brandy.
HUSBAND: No.
WIFE: I repeat: give me a glass of brandy.
HUSBAND: You won't get another drop today.
WIFE: Then I'll get it myself.
HUSBAND: Stop making scenes. You know I won't let you drink today. You can't let your son's kidnapping be another excuse to get drunk. Besides, we don't know what else might happen today. We might need you to do something.
WIFE: *(softly)* You haven't needed me for a long time. It takes a disaster for you to say you do.
HUSBAND: *(businesslike)* I don't think they'll phone again today. They try to wear us down by keeping us on tenterhooks. And one other thing: when Kasia comes in the morning you mustn't breathe a word of this.

WIFE: *(surprised, but resigned)* All right.

HUSBAND: We'll sit up for a bit longer, then have some supper and…

WIFE: I'm not hungry. *(Almost shouting)* I can't even think about food! Can't you understand that?

HUSBAND: You ought to have something to eat. You need to be ready. After supper you can go to bed. I'll stay by the phone. We can change over after a few hours… Or maybe not. We can both go to bed. The phone will be by my bed.

WIFE: You're in your element, aren't you? *(Sniggering)* Planning, deployment, superb organization… You're so funny.

HUSBAND: Possibly. But my son's life is at stake. Being sentimental won't get us far. We have to act.

WIFE: All right, all right… Before… Before that phone call you said Stan was well aware of certain things… What did you mean?

HUSBAND: On one or two occasions when you came home barely conscious, he carried you upstairs. And once he asked if your lovers weren't enough and if you really had to drink so much as well. You tried to smack his face but you fell down on the floor.

(Silence, sound of breathing)

WIFE: Tomorrow morning I'll give that vixen her notice. I'll do it first thing.

HUSBAND: No you won't. In the first place, where would you find a cleaner as good as her, and in the second, I won't let you. She had a moral obligation to tell me. She asked my advice. She was deeply shocked. She's a religious person. She has principles… She's been with us so many years that she feels it deeply. After all she feels she's a member of the family.

WIFE: The vixen, bearing tittle-tattle.

HUSBAND: Why do you always blame other people, never yourself?

WIFE: Speak for yourself.

HUSBAND: I've admitted my guilt. Partial guilt. But you don't want to remember that.

WIFE: I don't remember… It must have been a long time ago.

HUSBAND: Yes, it was.

WIFE: And after that we stopped talking, except for set phrases.

HUSBAND: That's a kind of companionship. Quite a tolerable kind, even.

WIFE: Not for me… Don't you realize I'm the kind of woman who wanted and still wants to get something out of life?

HUSBAND: I realize that all too well.

WIFE: Is that why you found less and less time for me and didn't see me as a wife, a physical body, or a person? You plunged into your bloody science and turned me into an object. Rather like that table... Well, I wanted to be a person for other people... Or a body, at least.

HUSBAND: I'm not blaming you. You don't have to make excuses.

WIFE: Of course you're not blaming me. You're above all that... Your little secretaries and postgraduate girls will give you a few minutes of pleasure, and everything else is at the Olympic level: achievements, successes... Of course you don't blame me.

HUSBAND: What do you want to do now?

WIFE: When?

HUSBAND: When this is all over. When we get him back.

WIFE: I don't know... *(Softly)* I suppose I've stuffed up my life. If I drink it's because that time between five and seven isn't enough for me.

HUSBAND: Do you want a divorce?

(Pause)

WIFE: No.

HUSBAND: Why not?

WIFE: *(expressionlessly)* Because I love you.

HUSBAND: Hmm. Words, words, words.

WIFE: Can't you see that inside me – a middle-aged woman – there's still the same young girl who used to put her arms round you and was blind to everything in the world but you?

HUSBAND: And you think we could still...?

WIFE: *(fiercely)* Yes, yes I do! *(After pause, softly)* Thank you. It's so long since you stroked my hair.

(Sound of door opening. Footsteps. Silence)

WIFE: *(shouting)* Stan! They've let you go!

STAN: Well, yes...

WIFE: *(in tears)* Stan!

HUSBAND: You'll suffocate him.

STAN: Come on, don't be silly, Mum.

WIFE: *(sobbing)* My son, my son...

HUSBAND: *(soothingly)* Sophie, Sophie.

WIFE: Sit down and tell us what happened.

HUSBAND: Wait a moment. Can't you see how upset he is?

STAN: I wanted to apologize. There was no kidnapping. It was all my idea. My friend was calling from a phone booth, and he had my voice recorded on this tape-recorder that I got from you... I wanted to draw it out a bit longer, but I couldn't.

WIFE: I don't understand. *(Angrily)* Why did you do it?

(Footsteps; the sound of a slap)

STAN: Hit me on the other cheek, Dad.
HUSBAND: Why did you do it?
STAN: *(rather sheepishly)* I… I wanted you two to have some respect for me. *(More softly)* And for yourselves.

(Cuckoo clock strikes eight)

THE GARDEN GATE

MOTHER: That's the seventeenth time you've washed your hands today.

SON: Mother, please!

MOTHER: I've been counting. Seventeen times. You've been to the toilet five times and flicked through eight magazines, reading a bit here and a bit there.

SON: When you moved in with me you promised you wouldn't make a nuisance of yourself.

MOTHER: Cecil dear, am I such a nuisance to you? How can an old woman in an armchair be a nuisance? If I sometimes rattle some pans in the kitchen, is that so awful? It's like when the radio plays one of those twanging, burbling, jangling tunes that you call music.

SON: Mother, you know what I mean.

MOTHER: (*after pause*) Yes, I think I do. I'm not supposed to take any notice of your little idiosyncrasies, but unfortunately, my dear, they're becoming more and more apparent… Just think: it's not yet noon, and although you had a shower when you got up you've washed your hands seventeen times… But then, even as a child you had a taste for poetic antics. For instance, you liked to go out into the garden through the window instead of the door, because you said the garden was completely different when you went out through the window. You were also fond of reciting monotonous counting rhymes when you could have been playing with your friends. But that had to do with your age. Now, though,…

SON: I had hoped to get some work done today, but you're deliberately annoying me.

MOTHER: Then why didn't you sit down at the typewriter straight after breakfast? I put some paper and carbon neatly in the typewriter for you. All you have to do is sit down… and write.

SON: What about?

MOTHER: Aha, you've nothing to write about. That's why you've washed your hands seventeen times.

SON: Don't you see that…

MOTHER: Yes, I do see. My poor little Cecil feels all empty inside… But don't worry, it'll pass. There'll be lots of events, maybe a new love, and news from the social scene, if that's what you call those endless intrigues in your circle of friends. Somebody will provide inspiration and everything will be fine. And you'll start tapping away again.

SON: I may not be able to, Mother.

MOTHER: That wouldn't be too serious either. You have your private means, plus whatever you make by editing for all those editorial committees or whatever those sinecures are called. You don't have to worry about your income.

SON: Sometimes I think you despise me.

MOTHER: Despise my one and only beloved son?

SON: Of course, you'd privately call it inspiration… Inspiring by annoying.

MOTHER: You're touching your eyelid. That nervous tic in your eye won't stop… Aren't you taking any vitamin B or those tranquillisers? You know, don't you, that that tic in your eyelid is a symptom of nervous exhaustion? I had the same thing after Dusia died.

SON: I am taking them.

MOTHER: So they don't help.

SON: That's how it looks.

MOTHER: None of those pills did me any good either after Dusia died… The only thing that helped was time… It'll pass for you too.

SON: But I haven't experienced anything very dramatic recently.

MOTHER: You're run down, exhausted.

SON: Nothing particular has happened to me.

MOTHER: That's the point: nothing particular. Tedium, anxiety as you reach the age when men start feeling they're getting old. Some turn to drink, go out hunting, burn themselves out in a fever of chaotic activity, explaining it, of course, by a need to do something for humanity. Others play cards, travel, trade their wives in for younger ones, and so on and so forth… But you, apart from a few gatherings with those friends, you're a bit of a loner… A little dalliance sometimes, what you call 'love', without much conviction… You don't need strong sensations. You don't like them. You just stay on your own and don't quite know what to do. Perhaps you ought to get married. An old woman like me is no company for a man who needs a bit of youthful freshness to relax… You ought to get married… You've got a big enough flat. I would go home to the country.

SON: Don't be silly. I'd miss you.

MOTHER: Yes, you would. But you'd have something else… You ought to marry somebody like Dusia.

SON: Are you going to start that again?

MOTHER: Have you got anything better to do this morning? Of course, you can go to your room, sit down at the typewriter and stare at the sheet of paper in it. After an hour you can tap one of the keys. A 'one' will appear at the top of the page. Then silence again… Or you could turn on the TV. In a minute they'll be showing an old western, the kind where the sheriff is a goodie and the bandit a baddie.

SON: What's for lunch?

MOTHER: Roast and salad. That should be enough for you… You've put on an amazing amount of weight in the last few months.

SON: And you've been losing weight.

MOTHER: I can assure you, my dear Cecil, that wizened old harridans are much more interesting than stout, spreading ones.

SON: There's a fire eating you. The fiendish fire of incapacity.

MOTHER: And what might I be yearning for, my dear boy? Incapacity is not a curse of old age but one of its privileges. You have so much time to think and twiddle your thumbs.

SON: So you take out all your spite on me.

MOTHER: That's obviously untrue… I like talking to you, because I know you need to talk… I'm the only one you can talk frankly to. Only from me will you hear a grain of truth or a bit of ironic rhetoric and be sure that it's coming from a friend… Isn't that so?

SON: Yes. But you're abusing your power.

MOTHER: An old lady's harmless bit of fun.

SON: Which I can deprive you of.

MOTHER: How?

SON: I could disappear, Mother. Just disappear.

MOTHER: Have you been offered some job abroad?… Or are you planning a long journey?

SON: Wherever I went, I'd have to take you with me.

MOTHER: Aha, my old Cecil is coming back to life. A bit of repartee. Bravo!… So you might disappear. Hmmm… You're not saying you might… Having Dusia kill herself was bad enough.

SON: Then you'd be completely alone.

MOTHER: I'm not the one that matters. You know, you ought to move to the country and re-train as a farmer.

SON: Can you really see me as some sort of moonstruck greenie, tilling the soil, listening to the birds singing, talking to streams and eating only natural products? I have a home in the city, and enough money to live comfortably. And if I want some fresh air I can suck a peppermint or go and stay in a boarding house.

MOTHER: In that case, my brave lad, you might as well hang yourself.

SON: Not a nice form of death, Mother.

MOTHER: It's no good being pernickety. We're not talking about some kind of baby food – pulped rice or spinach. If there's no other medicine, you have to close your eyes and swallow it... But you also need to have some feeling of unhappiness. And you don't suffer from that.

SON: I do. When I lose at poker.

MOTHER: Your friends used to say that when you were a student – how many years ago? Heavens! twenty-three, twenty-four – you lived at a hectic pace. A rage to live, all sorts of schemes, feverish work, late nights, compulsive reading... You were on fire.

SON: And I burnt out.

MOTHER: The life went out of you.

SON: It'd be embarrassing if I hadn't changed.

MOTHER: 'The life went out of you' is an understatement. You are dead. Sometimes your limbs still jerk, like a dead frog when you put an electric pulse through it, but in reality you're dead... Still, you really don't need to wash your hands seventeen times in one morning. They really aren't as dirty as that. Didn't you ever do anything worse?

SON: No, actually I didn't... I only started too early and it's just too easy to be influenced.

MOTHER: We can't all be made of iron... It's mostly half-wits who are.

SON: But not only half-wits.

MOTHER: Not only, of course. But you were never made of the stuff of saints or heroes.

SON: Sometimes I thought I might be.

MOTHER: Just youthful illusions.

SON: I've lost the feeling...

MOTHER: You're not trying to tell me about self-respect or a feeling of masculinity. Even if in your books you might describe somebody like you as having had 'his balls cut off', in that crudely robust style of yours. It has nothing in common with the truth... And on the subject of masculinity, weren't you once going to tell me about a memory that you couldn't shake off? It had something to do with your first girlfriend.

SON: (*after pause*) She liked running her fingers through my hair while we were lying side by side. I used to flinch. I was so young that I was ashamed of any tenderness. Years later I used to recall the motion of her hand, the movement of my hair, the tingling sensation in my scalp.

MOTHER: How romantic... A nice angle on your wild youth.

SON: I realize full well that I'm disgustingly normal now. But isn't that the worst form of insanity?

MOTHER: Nicely put. You shouldn't lose hope: in a while you'll write some new moralizing piece.
SON: It seems to me you're a cynic.
MOTHER: Somebody has to be the man about the house.
SON: Then I'll go and…
MOTHER: Sit still, you don't have to wash your hands for the eighteenth time…
SON: I wanted to go to the kitchen and bring you some wine.
MOTHER: Good idea, Cecil darling.

(*Footsteps. Sound of old lady humming. Footsteps returning*)

SON: Here you are.
MOTHER: Thank you, dear. Won't you have any?
SON: Mother, you know about my liver…
MOTHER: I'm sorry, dear, I'm getting sclerotic. I keep forgetting… It's very nice wine. Light, with body.
SON: Would you like to go to the cinema with me?
MOTHER: I'd rather stay at home. But you go if you like. Just hold on half an hour and have some lunch… But, to return to what we were talking about, will you be getting married?
SON: To someone like Dusia, right?
MOTHER: Oh, that was just something I said… She doesn't have to be like Dusia at all… I just meant you need a change in your life.
SON: And then you'd move out.
MOTHER: If you'd like me to stay, I would. But I might be a nuisance.
SON: I don't want to marry anybody.
MOTHER: Then try to change something in your life. Shake off the past! Do something revolutionary, by your own standards, like walking into one of those editorial offices of yours on your hands.
SON: I wouldn't be able to walk on my hands.
MOTHER: Paint your face like an Indian on the warpath.
SON: (*with an approving sigh*) Oh, Mother…
MOTHER: Believe me, darling, what you need is a good jolt. Otherwise things will go badly for you. You really will be lifeless – it won't just be my teasing expression.
SON: You know, since Dusia died, not even my own aspirations have meant much to me. When I had her with me, I wanted to do something worthwhile. I had someone to do things for.
MOTHER: I see. And now you've only got me.
SON: Don't misunderstand me.
MOTHER: I understand you very well. You don't need to explain.
SON: Then I just became a kind of process worker. I took orders and filled them… Dusia saw me as an artist, a person and a brave man… I was

different with her… I know she was a bit naive, but the kind of faith she had in me means so much in life… It helps you believe in yourself. (*Pause*) Even if that belief in yourself is self-deception.

MOTHER: Even now you're deceiving yourself, my boy… Dusia's death was a very handy pretext for you to accept yourself as you were. 'My beloved wife has killed herself, so I can now luxuriate in inertia.' And you really can be attached to that inertia. It frees you from so many decisions, so much trouble… Isn't that so, Cecil?

SON: You can see it that way… But I still think Dusia's departure was also the culmination of a certain process…

MOTHER: Meaning?

SON: The process of my surrendering to my surroundings.

MOTHER: Go on.

SON: … as well as the disappearance of the one person who really loved me.

MOTHER: And you, my dear Cecil, are the one who says that Dusia was naive! You're wonderfully naive yourself.

SON: What are you talking about, Mother?

MOTHER: Nothing in particular.

SON: Are you trying to suggest that Dusia didn't love me?

MOTHER: Of course she loved you. That word can stand for so many different emotional and psychological states… You needed her, in any case. You needed her just the way she seemed to you.

SON: Mother, you don't mean to say Dusia wasn't the way she seemed, that she was only pretending.

MOTHER: It shouldn't matter that much to you now, nearly six years after her death… Anyway, you have others to take a lead from now, because you probably always need somebody to lean on. I don't mean me. I simply fill a certain need you have for psychological comfort. I'm a sort of counsellor cum clown to you. The kind you lean on – all those friends of yours who come here sometimes – all have one thing in common, whatever their background: they're self-confident, they charge straight ahead, seizing for themselves everything that's rightfully theirs – in their view, of course. They're the kind you need. Strong and uncompromising. You feel safe with them, you defer to them. But they also need you. People like them need to have weaker souls around them, whom they can make use of, and who don't threaten them. So they share things with you, pass you things they themselves can't swallow.

SON: Everything I have is thanks to my own efforts.

MOTHER: You have all your sinecures and privileges thanks to your acquaintances. And that has nothing to do with the fact that you're a writer. If you were an engineer, a director, a doctor or a scientist, nothing would be any different, because – if it sounds old-fashioned –

you're a weak man... (*Pause*) But I wouldn't want it any other way, Cecil... I like weak, sensitive souls. To me, that's the best thing about the human race, it's what raises us above the level of animals. That's why I'd like you to find a wife who'd bring you a bit of youthful freshness. Of course I'd want to have a look at the fresh young thing beforehand. I haven't much faith in your judgement of women, although all your heroines are very complex characters... Oh look, this is my third glass. You're free to call me an alcoholic.

SON: I think you'd like to be one of those who charges straight ahead.

MOTHER: Heavens! We all have to die anyway, so why burden yourself with ambitions? You'll live to a ripe old age and be revered as a classic while all those macho intriguers, go-getters and tanks in human clothing are six feet under, brought down by heart attacks, devoured by stomach ulcers... My husband was one of those. He was appointed professor early but didn't have long to enjoy it. He died a splendid death, though, like Catherine the Great, on the lavatory.

SON: Whatever would I do without you, you old brute?

MOTHER: You'd get bored.

SON: That's for sure.

MOTHER: I provide a bit of tension. I tease you and scold you, and in a way I'm proud of you, that is, in my way, I love you. And you provide suitable maintenance, and that allows you to feel you're a kind person, that is, you're satisfying your own need for psychological comfort... I'd be bored without you too, probably half to death... Because you mean life to me.

SON: When you called me in here you said you had a surprise for me.

MOTHER: I wanted to entice you here.

SON: No, no. I can tell you're hiding something.

MOTHER: I'd had enough of your hand-washing. I thought a little adversarial banter would do you good.

SON: I know you better. There was something in your voice that told me...

MOTHER: (*after pause*) All right. If you absolutely have to know... Tell me first, but in all sincerity: why did Dusia decide to do what she did?

SON: We know all about that. Shock at losing a child.

MOTHER: Miscarriage can cause breakdowns, of course... I have here a letter from her, written just before she died. Would you like me to read some of it to you?

SON: She wrote to you? You didn't say anything about it.

MOTHER: I'm telling you now. I think the time has come. Shall I read you some of it?

(*Silence*)

MOTHER: If you don't want me to...
SON: (*hurriedly*) Go on then.
MOTHER: Right. Where did I put my glasses?
SON: On the table.
MOTHER: Thank you. (*Reads*) 'Dearest Mummy,' (*rapid, indistinct whisper*). Ah, here we are. 'As for Cec, he played his part in it too, but not like Stefan and the others. He did it just by being so stupid. I'd come home warmed by other men's bodies and he wouldn't even notice, or didn't want to notice. I had to play the devoted idiot and talk about boring things that seemed to matter to him. I had to force myself, as I did all my life with all the other men, but with him it was incredibly boring. The fool was so glad about the child we were going to have, which was Stefan's child, that it made me want to throw up and weep at once, for myself and him. It was horrible, horrible, horrible.' (*Pause*) The rest of it's nothing to do with you.
SON: Will you show it to me?
MOTHER: My daughter was a neurotic slut. Perhaps it was my fault, perhaps not... And you're a good boy. Ordinary and good. These days we're ashamed to use the word, but it exists. Although I was your mother-in-law you started calling me 'Mother', and that's what I became... My own daughter was an empty, pitiful, neurotic slut. My own daughter... So you became my true son. My real son.
SON: Give me that letter.
MOTHER: Here you are... You once told me that when you were a child you liked going out into the garden through the window, because that made the garden different... This letter can be your window, my son.

QUADRAPHONY

(*Voices speaking in a whisper. Volume swelling and fading by turns. Words indistinct. The sweet tones of a flute drown out the whispers. Then a sudden crash of drums, a clash of sounding brass, then silence.*)

FEMALE VOICE I: All trussed up and tied to a revolving chair…

MALE VOICE II: All trussed up, all trussed up…

MALE VOICE III: (*sniggers*) Trussed up like a lamb for the slaughter.

FEMALE VOICE IV: And no doors in the walls.

FEMALE VOICE I: If you use your feet to turn the chair, you'll be able to see us…

MALE VOICE II: He's turned with his chair.

MALE VOICE III: His eyes look blind, although he can see.

FEMALE VOICE IV: He stopped it turning by dragging his heels on the floor.

FEMALE VOICE I: You see the loudspeakers. One in each corner.

MALE VOICE II: Quadraphonic.

MALE VOICE III: (*chuckling*) But we can see you.

FEMALE VOICE IV: Wallpaper on the walls, covered in eyes… Four pairs of those eyes belong to us… Among hundreds of others.

FEMALE VOICE I: As a child you turned your back on your mother.

MALE VOICE II: She abandoned you, your brother, your sister and your father.

MALE VOICE III: (*ironically*) She followed the call of her body.

FEMALE VOICE IV: Among the eyes on the wall you can see her eyes… She used to bend over you when you were ill, and you would touch her breast with your childish hand.

FEMALE VOICE I: That's something you wanted to forget … that and the smell of her hands. They smelt of cosmetics, and something else that made you inwardly shudder.

MALE VOICE II: You tried to forget, but you couldn't.

MALE VOICE III: You didn't want to talk to her when she came visiting. (*Chuckling*) 'You're not my mother,' you yelled, and looked to your father for approval.

FEMALE VOICE IV: And in the holidays you lay down in a meadow and rubbed your face in the sweet grass and warm earth, and called it 'mother'.

FEMALE VOICE I: You dreamed about that meadow when you went back to the city.

MALE VOICE II: You often dreamed of it later, when you weren't a child any more.

MALE VOICE III: (*sarcastically*) When you had an education behind you, you knew all about psychoanalysis, and tried to rationalize your dreams.

FEMALE VOICE IV: It was no good. You went on missing them.

FEMALE VOICE I: Cut off from your father the office-worker, your sports-mad brother and sex-machine sister, cut off by a thousand miles although you all lived in the same crowded flat, you roamed dark jungles and the cities of the moon as you climbed mountains of printed words.

MALE VOICE II: Cut off from the earth.

MALE VOICE III: (*in tones of pseudo-scholarship*) Metaphorically speaking, from your mother.

FEMALE VOICE IV: The cloud of imagination could no longer bear your weight when you became conscious of your own body. The body of a growing boy.

FEMALE VOICE I: You came down to an asphalt-covered earth, where there were girls walking and smelling of the sweetness of warm grass.

MALE VOICE II: Your rapid breathing.

MALE VOICE III: You weren't too confident with girls. They preferred better talkers. Boys who had the gift of the gab. While you just stammered and blushed.

FEMALE VOICE IV: Until one day, in a meadow outside town, a gentle, protective girl took you in hand.

FEMALE VOICE I: You came back down to earth.

MALE VOICE II: You found your mother.

MALE VOICE III: (*laughing*) You stopped dreaming about far-off lands and outer space, and started dreaming about… hee, hee, hee!

FEMALE VOICE IV: You came home proud of your initiation, and humbled by the miracle of that inner flash of lightning, that moment when you glimpsed the world as a whole.

FEMALE VOICE I: Young and self-assured, you knew you were experiencing a moment of revelation, that women, animals, flowers, houses and birds were all pebbles in one grand mosaic. Words seemed too unambiguous to describe that elaborate whole. There was no paint bright enough to express the brilliance of that revelation. You realized that music was the medium that came closest to the heart of things and feelings.

MALE VOICE II: You studied music so diligently.

MALE VOICE III: Not forgetting the girls at the conservatoire.

FEMALE VOICE IV: You shone at young composers' contests. Lithe and strong, with a winning smile and a future that reached out before you like a shining pathway.

FEMALE VOICE I: You strode the earth with the step of a conqueror.

MALE VOICE II: Never turning to look at anybody.

MALE VOICE III: (*sniggers*) Putting it plainly, a selfish bastard.

FEMALE VOICE IV: Composing gave you physical pleasure.

FEMALE VOICE I: Your colours were bright, the scents powerful, the touch delicate, your ear faultless, and your taste so rich, so rich...

MALE VOICE II: Women gave themselves to you and vanished, replaced by others.

MALE VOICE III: (*laughing*) Sometimes the idiot was quite sure he'd never die.

FEMALE VOICE IV: As an artist he changed. He was more and more self-confident. He could see the path he had to follow. In the far distance, masterpieces rose like trees by the roadside. Unique. Inimitable.

FEMALE VOICE I: You were invited to perform your compositions. You got to see new countries. Landscapes opened before you like women. You were quick to possess them with all your five senses. Most of all you loved Mediterranean landscapes, with soil open to the sun and green so different from the piercing green of the north.

MALE VOICE II: You went happily to sleep, sated by the sun.

MALE VOICE III: (*sniggers*) And of course, by this time you had no dreams at all.

FEMALE VOICE IV: You were so happy, so happy.

FEMALE VOICE I: You started composing a quartet, 'The Four Elements'.

MALE VOICE II: The four parts were called Earth, Air, Fire and Water.

MALE VOICE III: Commissioned by the Geller Foundation. For a tidy sum in dollars.

FEMALE VOICE IV: You worked at it in the country. In a little cottage in the depths of a forest.

FEMALE VOICE I: You worked out your own notation system. You got up early, bathed in the bracing water of the lake, jumped out, did some exercises – filled with wonder at your own fitness – then, when you'd warmed up, you would hurry into your cottage, drink a cup of coffee and get down to work.

MALE VOICE II: In a state of inspiration.

MALE VOICE III: (*laughing*) In those days you believed in yourself.

FEMALE VOICE IV: At midday you got your own lunch, ate it with relish and went for a walk in the forest.

FEMALE VOICE I: You used to talk to the trees, the clouds, the birds and the little rabbits… You called them 'Brother Tree', 'Sister Cloud' and 'Brer Rabbit', like Saint Francis.

MALE VOICE II: You liked the feel of that springy moss under your feet. The air scented with pine. The columns of light in the forest.

MALE VOICE III: (*laughing out loud*) You were so very pleased with yourself.

FEMALE VOICE IV: You would go out into a sunny glade and lie down in the scented herbs.

FEMALE VOICE I: Listening to the insects.

MALE VOICE II: Gazing at the clouds sailing across the sky.

MALE VOICE III: Part of nature, you might say.

FEMALE VOICE IV: At one with the earth.

FEMALE VOICE I: You finished your quartet. On the last day you worked for nearly twenty hours non-stop.

MALE VOICE II: You went out into the forest. Exhausted. Inwardly drained. But happy.

MALE VOICE III: (*laughing*) Your first steps on the slippery slope.

FEMALE VOICE IV: The earth rose up and hit you.

FEMALE VOICE I: You fainted, then came to and saw an ant.

MALE VOICE II: So close to your eye that it looked like a monster.

MALE VOICE III: (*laughing*) 'Mummy!' you groaned.

FEMALE VOICE IV: You got to your feet, with a Chinese gong pounding in your aching head.

FEMALE VOICE I: There in the forest you turned your back on the earth.

MALE VOICE II: You shouted out loud that you didn't want to see it, that you wanted to fly.

MALE VOICE III: A dramatic moment… Or a squalid attack of hysteria.

FEMALE VOICE IV: You couldn't express what you felt, but even without words you realized what it was.

FEMALE VOICE I: You went home to the city, had a copy made of 'The Four Elements', and sent it to the Foundation.

MALE VOICE II: You didn't go to the world premiere performance.

MALE VOICE III: (*tittering*) Too busy with your own feelings. Listening to your own inner self.

FEMALE VOICE IV: You lived as you did before, but you were different.

FEMALE VOICE I: The women sensed it first. They weren't as quick to oblige as they used to be, although you seemed eager enough. They sensed that you weren't really interested.

MALE VOICE II: Even though you put everything into it.

MALE VOICE III: (*laughing*) You didn't understand yourself, you poor little thing. You seemed to be in a daze.

FEMALE VOICE IV: You were sent a recording of 'The Four Elements'.

FEMALE VOICE I: You listened over and over again.

MALE VOICE II: You hardly went out of the house.

MALE VOICE III: (*gleefully*) Stopped taking care of yourself. You avoided soap and water. You didn't smell too sweet, my dear.

FEMALE VOICE IV: Once when you couldn't sleep you noticed the eyes on the wallpaper.

FEMALE VOICE I: Watching you intently.

MALE VOICE II: One particular pair of eyes.

MALE VOICE III: (*gaily*) Shining. Luminous.

FEMALE VOICE IV: You pulled the covers over your head. But you could still see those eyes through them.

FEMALE VOICE I: You jumped out of bed and turned on the tape-recorder.

MALE VOICE II: Part One of 'The Four Elements': Earth.

(*Music distorted by the running of the tape. Grotesque sounding voices, lasting for about a minute, becoming unbearable*)

MALE VOICE II: How nice the Latin words of 'The Four Elements' sound!

MALE VOICE III: (*gloating*) Lovely!

FEMALE VOICE IV: The eyes disappeared. There was only music.

MALE VOICE I: It bore you upward like a kite in the breeze.

MALE VOICE II: High above the earth you could let yourself be lulled in the gentle air. Everything down below looked tiny.

FEMALE VOICE III: Insignificant.

FEMALE VOICE IV: Aesthetic. Pastel quilt blotches of fields. The starry patches of towns.

FEMALE VOICE I: But when the music faded, you were back on earth.

MALE VOICE II: That nagging awareness of being flesh and blood. And fragile bones.

MALE VOICE III: (*happily*) Pathological hypersensitivity.

FEMALE VOICE IV: Even in young bodies you saw the progress of decay.

FEMALE VOICE I: The skin of those bodies became transparent. The pumping heart became a horrible sort of clock.

MALE VOICE II: The newspapers, radio and television were instruments of torture. You were crushed by falling walls during earthquakes, you perished in car accidents, you were torn by bullets in distant wars, pumped full of morphine to die of cancer, interrogated by all the police forces of the world until you betrayed your comrades, forced to silence by tyrants until you could only utter a soundless yelp, you drowned in floods and died of thirst in deserts…

MALE VOICE III: Even fine weather only served to remind you that you were mortal.

FEMALE VOICE IV: He tried to fight it.

FEMALE VOICE I: He appealed to common sense for help.

MALE VOICE II: He wanted to be like everybody else. He knew he'd go mad if he got involved in so much suffering.

MALE VOICE III: (*mimicking*) 'Time to be realistic,' he used to say.

FEMALE VOICE IV: He decided to change his way of life.

FEMALE VOICE I: Plenty of activity. Regular hours of sleep.

MALE VOICE II: Keeping busy. He took a job as a teacher in a music school. Organized festivals of music. Sat on committees, was active at association meetings, spoke on radio and TV about music. Gave interviews. An energetic spokesman for the arts, the professional perfectionist and popularizer.

MALE VOICE III: And so well dressed. Never showy. Never sloppy. Being an artist, he didn't need to dress like one. His suits had just the right conservative touch, and the colour scheme was flawless. Sharp creases in his trousers. Shoes polished so you could see your reflection. Snow-white shirt. Scrubbed clean. Delicately scented. He washed his hands scores of times a day.

FEMALE VOICE IV: His flat was spotless.

FEMALE VOICE I: He would speak contemptuously to his students about artists who turned for inspiration to drugs, metaphysics and exotic cultures that you couldn't absorb properly without being born into them.

MALE VOICE II: He spoke with conviction. He taught them to beware of bullshit. He made fun of it in his public statements, pointing out ornamental borrowings. He praised common sense.

MALE VOICE III: (*tittering*) But he didn't turn his back on what he called 'so-called inspiration'… He wasn't as crazy as that… He even said that so-called inspiration could be compared to a religious state of grace.

FEMALE VOICE IV: Young people looked up to him. The boys wanted to be just like him. The girls transposed his pedagogical statements into the language of love.

FEMALE VOICE I: He composed… Yes, he went on composing… The critics wrote that he was evolving, but he knew that he was just recycling his old ideas.

MALE VOICE II: But that didn't bother him.

MALE VOICE III: (*laughing*) He was deceiving himself, saying to himself that you had to work new ground to the limit.

FEMALE VOICE IV: He married a beautiful, intelligent woman.

FEMALE VOICE I: He decided to have two children.

MALE VOICE II: Their friends said his wife was of the same psychological type. She had good judgement and was embarrassed by any rapturous excesses.

MALE VOICE III: (*sniggering*) Except the kind they had in bed. But that's only natural. (*Mimicking*) Biological urges.

FEMALE VOICE IV: They both disliked unbalanced people and people who were too emotional. They couldn't stand pretentious flim-flam, the kind that seemed to be searching but was really so much hot air.

FEMALE VOICE I: They were afraid of people like that, although they didn't like to admit it to themselves.

MALE VOICE II: Perhaps he was the only one who was afraid. Maybe she saw it as a tiresome convention.

MALE VOICE III: Yes, he was afraid to glance into the abyss. (*Gleefully*) In case he felt dizzy… And he might have seen something hideous at the bottom.

FEMALE VOICE IV: Your first child was born at exactly the time you had planned.

FEMALE VOICE I: Your behaviour was exemplary. Sensitive to the mother's needs, delighted with the baby.

MALE VOICE II: You discovered that the body can be an instrument producing its own delightful music. As you watched your wife with the baby at her breast, you flew high above the earth. Lofted like a kite by a breath of wind. The earth sailed on beneath you, with blurred outlines, like a bouquet of flowers as seen by somebody with short sight.

MALE VOICE III: You came back to earth. For example, when you refused a loan to an old college friend who'd struck a patch of bad luck… And he didn't escape a homily about the need to work hard and keep on working. And you had the base satisfaction of seeing him masochistically agreeing.

FEMALE VOICE IV: You and your wife got on so well.

FEMALE VOICE I: Sometimes you voiced the same thought at the same time.

MALE VOICE II: Sometimes, when you looked at her, you wondered if she knew.

MALE VOICE III: That all your hard work and tidy-mindedness was a kind of defence mechanism.

FEMALE VOICE IV: But no, she had no suspicions.

FEMALE VOICE I: She felt safe with you.

MALE VOICE II: She was so trusting.

MALE VOICE III: Petty bourgeois happiness… A successful marriage, a healthy baby, and a doctorate close to completion about the depiction of demons in folk art… Hee, hee, hee!

FEMALE VOICE IV: No, she didn't suspect anything.

FEMALE VOICE I: You gave her no cause. To her you seemed a rock of ages. A man of real character. Almost a kind of engineer of life, keeping control of life as well as sound. And your being an artist was an added adornment to your marriage. It was all in the best of taste.

MALE VOICE II: Occasionally you had the feeling that everything you did and everything that happened around you was unreal.

MALE VOICE III: You were right.

FEMALE VOICE IV: You didn't want to think about that.

FEMALE VOICE I: You were becoming even busier than before. Finding more and more things to do.

MALE VOICE II: So you wouldn't have to think about it.

MALE VOICE III: (*laughing*) And you didn't think about it. Or so it seemed. But it was there at the back of your mind, festering away…

FEMALE VOICE IV: Until it flared up. And you realized again…

FEMALE VOICE I: How unreal your life was.

MALE VOICE II: You knew that your neat and tidy home, model marriage, regular habits and hard work were all a castle in the air for you to sail in, high above the earth.

MALE VOICE III: (*laughing out loud*) The frightening earth.

FEMALE VOICE IV: At the mercy of the air.

FEMALE VOICE I: You started noticing similarities with your 'Four Elements'. You compared the stages of your life to the composition.

MALE VOICE II: Auto-suggestion.

MALE VOICE III: (*cheerily*) There are those who say that thinking in analogies is the sign of a magician or an idiot.

FEMALE VOICE IV: Your self-confidence was deserting you.

FEMALE VOICE I: You were on the look-out for signs.

MALE VOICE II: Signs signalling the onset of a period of fire. You were wondering what kind of fire you'd have to walk through.

MALE VOICE III: Your imagination was working overtime.

FEMALE VOICE IV: Imagining all sorts of horrors. Thinking about them. Wondering how you'd cope.

FEMALE VOICE I: And after a while you felt sure there was no threat to you.

MALE VOICE II: That it was only auto-suggestion… That you were mechanically comparing your life to a musical composition.

MALE VOICE III: You laughed at yourself. Secretly, of course. So's not to worry the little woman.

FEMALE VOICE IV: And then, feeling sure of yourself, you realized you could do without music.

FEMALE VOICE I: You came to see it as your job. A trade… Nothing more.

MALE VOICE II: You joined with those who think the best form of music is silence.

MALE VOICE III: (*sniggers*) It seemed so innocent.

FEMALE VOICE IV: You used this discovery for your own pleasure. Before going to sleep you listened to the silence.

FEMALE VOICE I: It was so musically rich.

MALE VOICE II: You were borne aloft on currents of air.

MALE VOICE III: As pleased as Punch… Coming close to experiencing what some of those despised practitioners of Zen and other oriental fashions call Nirvana.

FEMALE VOICE IV: Yes, music that was written down and performed seemed pointless compared to silence.

FEMALE VOICE I: You stopped composing.

MALE VOICE II: You told your wife you were thinking of changing your style, so you needed some time out. She knew words like 'style' very well, so she understood at once and approved of your decision.

MALE VOICE III: The poor thing didn't know you'd tossed away your birthright.

FEMALE VOICE IV: Only one thing concerned her: you'd become so cold.

FEMALE VOICE I: She thought it was overwork. She didn't mention it. She was too tactful.

MALE VOICE II: You spoke less and less. You thought words were unnecessary.

(*Music distorted by the running of the tape. Grotesque voices, lasting for about a minute, becoming unbearable*)

MALE VOICE III: Part Two of your quartet: Air… (*sniggers*)

(*Sound of tape being rewound*)

FEMALE VOICE IV: More and more you avoided speaking… You listened to the silence… But that silence was no longer a raging fire of music… The flame was dying.

FEMALE VOICE I: Until it burned right out… There was no more music. You were listening to silence.

MALE VOICE II: You listened in vain… There was nothing but silence… All you could hear was silence.

MALE VOICE III: The young lecturer knew so many pieces of music… He tried to recall them… tried to bring them back… But he couldn't.

FEMALE VOICE IV: All he could hear was silence.

FEMALE VOICE I: Being unable to listen to recorded music, classical music, and feeling cheated by silence…

MALE VOICE II: … he became a pleasure-seeker.

MALE VOICE III: (*cheerily*) Threw restraint to the winds.

FEMALE VOICE IV: In the homes of lonely women, mostly divorcees, independent but desperately longing for company, desperately afraid of being alone…

FEMALE VOICE I: … he was charming… Talkative, lovable, disappearing only to reappear unexpectedly… A knight errant.

MALE VOICE II: He made them feel attractive and wanted, those women who were still young but conscious of growing older… They adored him. They had the illusion that there really was a race of happy people who lived without problems and lived only for pleasure.

MALE VOICE III: (*gleefully*) And oh! How hard he tried!… How much effort he put into it!

FEMALE VOICE IV: He found those games more and more tiresome.

FEMALE VOICE I: And became more and more bad-tempered with his wife.

MALE VOICE II: At the slightest provocation.

MALE VOICE III: (*laughing*) And how that child infuriated him!

FEMALE VOICE IV: That and his wife's love for it.

FEMALE VOICE I: His little daughter's questions and her vitality got to be unbearable.

MALE VOICE II: To avoid displaying his feelings, he resorted again to the well-tried method of silence.

MALE VOICE III: (*cheerily*) He would run away from home… Over a drink he'd get maudlin, thinking about how unworthy he was… The thought of his shabby treatment of his wife and daughter brought a teasing kind of pleasure.

FEMALE VOICE IV: From time to time he tried to show them some tenderness. But he soon lapsed into silence again when he saw his wife's mistrust for these sudden fits of sentiment and his daughter's fear of this paternal solicitude.

FEMALE VOICE I: Sometimes his silence was broken by a scream.

MALE VOICE II: His wife and child didn't sense that that scream was a cry for help. To them it was just a form of aggression.

MALE VOICE III: (*amused*) Yet those shouts really were a cry for help. They were.

FEMALE VOICE IV: His wife tried to understand why she no longer interested him sexually, why he was torturing her with his silence, why he would turn livid with sudden rage and emit those inarticulate cries.

FEMALE VOICE I: She put it down to the way her body had changed since the child was born, or to the artistic crisis her husband was going through, and found glib explanations in applied psychology.

MALE VOICE II: She still saw him as he had been before.

MALE VOICE III: (*sniggering*) Fit, energetic, protective, terrific.

FEMALE VOICE IV: And she thought all that would pass.

FEMALE VOICE I: She loved him.

MALE VOICE II: He knew that.

MALE VOICE III: So he tried to put an end to it… Oh so diabolically.

FEMALE VOICE IV: In the end she agreed…

FEMALE VOICE I: After they'd had several conversations… Did she still believe anything could change him, or did he awaken that other kind of curiosity?

MALE VOICE II: You sat in a corner and watched a scene involving your wife and two men.

MALE VOICE III: (*gaily*) And a little wood-carving of a folk demon. One that she'd brought back from a field-trip to the country.

FEMALE VOICE IV: You went out.

FEMALE VOICE I: You sat in a bar remembering the satisfied look on your wife's face.

MALE VOICE II: You felt in your guts the creeping flame of jealousy.

MALE VOICE III: (*laughing*) Humiliated.

FEMALE VOICE IV: Depressed.

FEMALE VOICE I: For weeks on end.

MALE VOICE II: You suddenly became talkative. You questioned your wife. Asked how many times she'd been unfaithful.

MALE VOICE III: (*sniggering*) The poor cheated husband.

FEMALE VOICE IV: She told you. Then she denied it. You demanded she tell you again, so she told you. You wanted the details, more and more details.

FEMALE VOICE I: Till at last, towards morning, you said you'd have to get a divorce.

MALE VOICE II: She didn't quite see what you were on about. She was falling asleep. She was tired.

MALE VOICE III: (*ironically*) Because since the business of the wooden demon you'd taken renewed interest in your wife.

FEMALE VOICE IV: You swapped your flat for two smaller ones.

FEMALE VOICE I: Your jealousy left you, along with your wife.

MALE VOICE II: You decorated your flat with part of your collection of folk demons.

MALE VOICE III: (*cheerily*) Your wife had given them to you for your new life.

FEMALE VOICE IV: You sometimes called on your lonely old girl-friends, but you weren't the same as you had been before.

FEMALE VOICE I: Alas, you couldn't any longer give them the feeling they were having a wonderful adventure.

MALE VOICE II: You sat facing them and feverishly tried to explain that everything around you was scorched by fire.

MALE VOICE III: (*laughing*) You bored them. And your groping was no more than a sad ritual.

FEMALE VOICE IV: One by one they dropped out of your life… With almost childish surprise you realized that they almost all wanted to have somebody permanent, that most of them already had someone, and that they didn't need you.

FEMALE VOICE I: You accepted loneliness as something natural. As your natural state.

MALE VOICE II: You performed your teaching duties mechanically and went home.

MALE VOICE III: To drink alone. (*Sniggers*)

FEMALE VOICE IV: But your organism couldn't absorb alcohol in large quantities. You were a bundle of raw nerves.

FEMALE VOICE I: Again you saw the eye. Shining. Luminous. One eye, then another, then more and more of them.

MALE VOICE II: You stopped drinking.

MALE VOICE III: (*with feigned sympathy*) Although you didn't see any visions, you began to be consumed by a fever of metaphysics. And that's even worse.

FEMALE VOICE IV: You walked the streets with that fever gnawing at you. Walking umpteen kilometres among crowds of people.

FEMALE VOICE I: Asking yourself questions that you'd never have uttered out loud in company.

MALE VOICE II: About the simplest and most important things.

MALE VOICE III: (*laughing out loud*) Pondering the poverty of the human condition.

FEMALE VOICE IV: Consumed by fire.

FEMALE VOICE I: Submitting to it.

MALE VOICE II: You thought it was purifying.

MALE VOICE III: (*chuckling*) The fool was used to thinking in clichés.

FEMALE VOICE IV: You had plenty of time to yourself. You'd dropped all those committee duties. You had only your teaching job.

FEMALE VOICE I: Gradually you came to know places where poverty and anger, fear and squalor meet and come together.

MALE VOICE II: You lingered there on your strolls.

MALE VOICE III: You sought them out.

FEMALE VOICE IV: Once or twice you were beaten up and mugged.
FEMALE VOICE I: Eventually those people accepted you.
MALE VOICE II: You became one of them.
MALE VOICE III: (*gleefully*) One of the cast-offs of the big city.
FEMALE VOICE IV: You joined in their escapades, saw how people could be abused, soaked up the spluttering rage, fear and ribaldry around you.
FEMALE VOICE I: The fire that was eating you flared up.
MALE VOICE II: Encircling your head.
MALE VOICE III: (*sniggering*) The poor sod thought he had some kind of anti-halo, an aura of evil.
FEMALE VOICE IV: He was considerate towards hysterical low-class women who were down on their luck.
FEMALE VOICE I: He spoke to them so nicely… They'd never heard anyone saying words like that before.
MALE VOICE II: He didn't spurn their grubby bodies.
MALE VOICE III: (*laughing*) A mollycoddled little intellectual keen to see the seamy side.
FEMALE VOICE IV: He would go home and play with his carved demons.
FEMALE VOICE I: But he was so restless he'd go out again, at night, into the country, and stand beneath the starry sky.
MALE VOICE II: And look up at it.
MALE VOICE III: (*cheerily*) And, being a tenth-rate comedian, recall Kant's words about the imperative that is in us and the starry sky above.
FEMALE VOICE IV: Strolling coatless on autumn nights…
FEMALE VOICE I: … when that inner flame made a coat unnecessary…
MALE VOICE II: … till he got ill.
MALE VOICE III: Got a dose of common or garden pneumonia, the idiot.
FEMALE VOICE IV: Lay in bed at home, all alone.
FEMALE VOICE I: Feeling he was on fire.
MALE VOICE II: He was happy.
MALE VOICE III: (*sniggers*) Probably humming one of the classics.
FEMALE VOICE IV: Heaved himself out of bed, and decided to burn his collection of demons.
FEMALE VOICE I: Wondered where the best place was to do it. The little gas stove was out of the question. He took the carvings into the bathroom and threw them into the bath…
MALE VOICE II: Poured in some meths and put a match to it.
MALE VOICE III: (*with feigned sympathy*) His very best friends!

FEMALE VOICE IV: Watching the flames creeping over the wooden demons and darkening the enamel of the bathtub, he felt like a flaming torch of terror himself.

FEMALE VOICE I: He didn't want to die.

MALE VOICE II: He wanted to live. He had to live.

MALE VOICE III: (*ironically*) He went back to the living room and phoned for an ambulance.

(*Music distorted by the running of the tape. Grotesque voices, lasting for about a minute, becoming unbearable*)

FEMALE VOICE IV: When he came out of hospital he started sleeping on his side with his knees drawn up.

FEMALE VOICE I: In foetal position.

MALE VOICE II: Immersed in the warm water of indifference.

MALE VOICE III: (*laughing*) Just shy of forty, and longing to be back in the womb.

FEMALE VOICE IV: He returned to his idea of passing through the four elements: earth, air, fire and water.

FEMALE VOICE I: He didn't know what might come afterwards.

MALE VOICE II: Immersed in the warm water of indifference, he waited for fulfilment.

MALE VOICE III: (*sniggers*) With a luxurious sense of being rid of all responsibility.

FEMALE VOICE IV: He went back to teaching. He spoke softly, seemed distant, and often sunk in his own thoughts.

FEMALE VOICE I: The students noticed that he'd changed. They felt uncomfortable with him.

MALE VOICE II: They felt they were getting in his way.

MALE VOICE III: His eyes looked blind, although he could see.

FEMALE VOICE IV: He visited his daughter, exchanged meaningless words with his ex-wife and her husband, and took the girl out for walks. She liked him the way he was now, with his timid manner and his smile.

FEMALE VOICE I: Usually they went to the zoo. There they separated. She liked standing and watching the monkeys playing in their cage, while he went to the aquarium and gazed at the fish swimming in it… Then he would meet her at the gate and take her home, stopping to buy some kind of present along the way.

MALE VOICE II: He read a lot. He became addicted to reading. Carried along by the cadences of prose like the currents of a river, he let time flow by.

MALE VOICE III: (*cheerily*) He plunged into his dreams as if they were water, and had dreams to match! Most often he was a sea creature swimming in the waters of the primeval ocean.

FEMALE VOICE IV: Living suspended in fluid composed of sleep, wakefulness, daydreams and stories from books he'd read.

FEMALE VOICE I: He watched television, listened to the radio, leafed through the papers. These were no longer instruments of torture. With streams of images and words flowing over him, he remained untouched, like some form of aquatic life.

MALE VOICE II: Occasionally he looked through some of his old compositions, amazed that he'd once been able to write them.

MALE VOICE III: (*with feigned sympathy*) The general view was that, as a composer, he was finished.

FEMALE VOICE IV: He knew what people were saying, but he didn't care.

FEMALE VOICE I: He found some letters that his former girlfriends had written to him. He read them, hardly able to believe he had once been the focus of love, pain, adoration, anger.

MALE VOICE II: The past had become blurred.

MALE VOICE III: There were only glinting lights in the fluid of memory, like the gleaming scales of a passing fish.

FEMALE VOICE IV: Once he tossed the torn scraps of letters down the toilet and looked at the blackened enamel of the bath… The burning of the demons seemed like a fragment of a book he had read.

FEMALE VOICE I: The holidays came round. He went to stay by the lake.

MALE VOICE II: He spent hours swimming.

MALE VOICE III: (*laughing*) When he got out and saw lovely women in swimming costumes he thought of fish.

FEMALE VOICE IV: Incapable of desire.

FEMALE VOICE I: All passion spent.

MALE VOICE II: Plunged in indifference.

MALE VOICE III: Waiting for someone to fish him out. Not believing in the Divine Fishing Rod, and having no faith in the net of humane concern for others, the poor sod waited to be fished out.

FEMALE VOICE IV: And he thought, without worrying, that that might mean death.

FEMALE VOICE I: He went home to the city. Passive. Gazing at the misty horizon.

MALE VOICE II: Reading day and night. Falling asleep with a book on his chest.

MALE VOICE III: (*laughing*) Lovely and clean! He did most of his reading in the bath.

FEMALE VOICE IV: Once he was woken by a thunderous roar. He was lying with his eyes open. He saw earth flying up into the air, and fire driven by the wind passing through the earth, and water filled the charred craters. He saw the four elements at war, and the roar of explosions, hurricanes, fires and cascades filled his ears. The elements combined produced a throbbing darkness.
FEMALE VOICE I: He lay in a sunlit room, staring at the wall.
MALE VOICE II: He saw the eyes.
MALE VOICE III: (*cheerily*) And heard us for the first time.
FEMALE VOICE IV: Our voices.
FEMALE VOICE I: We were talking to him.
MALE VOICE II: Telling him stories.
MALE VOICE III: Prompting him.
FEMALE VOICE IV: Voices, whispers, screams.
FEMALE VOICE I: He didn't want to listen. He ordered some wallpaper with hundreds of eyes on it.
MALE VOICE II: He felt as if he was sitting triumphantly in his wallpapered room.
MALE VOICE III: (*sniggers*) Thought he'd tricked us into disappearing.
FEMALE VOICE IV: We kept quiet.
FEMALE VOICE I: Until at last he called for us himself.
MALE VOICE II: Waiting for us was torture.
MALE VOICE III: (*laughing out loud*) He missed us so much.
FEMALE VOICE IV: But we were in no hurry.
FEMALE VOICE I: He cleared out all the furniture, leaving only his rotating armchair.
MALE VOICE II: And a quadraphonic tape-recorder.
MALE VOICE III: Wanted to call us up by magic.
FEMALE VOICE IV: He put on his tape of 'The Four Elements'.
FEMALE VOICE I: All trussed up and tied to a revolving chair…
MALE VOICE II: All trussed up, all trussed up…
MALE VOICE III: (*sniggers*) Trussed up like a lamb for the slaughter.
FEMALE VOICE IV: And no doors in the walls.
FEMALE VOICE I: If you use your feet to turn the chair, you'll be able to see us…
MALE VOICE II: He's turned with his chair.
MALE VOICE III: His eyes look blind, although he can see.
FEMALE VOICE IV: He stopped it turning by dragging his heels on the floor.
FEMALE VOICE I: You see the loudspeakers. One in each corner.
MALE VOICE II: Quadraphonic.
MALE VOICE III: (*chuckling*) But we can see you.

FEMALE VOICE IV: Wallpaper on the walls, covered in eyes... Four pairs of those eyes belong to us... Among hundreds of others.

FEMALE VOICE I: All trussed up by expectation...

MALE VOICE II: All trussed up, all trussed up...

MALE VOICE III: Like a lamb for the slaughter.

FEMALE VOICE IV: No doors in the walls because you don't need any.

FEMALE VOICE I: What now?

MALE VOICE II: What now?

MALE VOICE III: What now?

FEMALE VOICE IV: What?

(*Voices speaking in a whisper. Volume swelling and fading by turns. Words indistinct. The sweet tones of a flute drown out the whispers. Then a sudden crash of drums, a clash of sounding brass, then silence.*)

Biographical Notes

Wojciech Dąbrowski was born in Cracow in 1947. He first studied electronic engineering at Warsaw Polytechnic before turning to the study of anthropology, which he studied at Warsaw University and later at the Australian National University in Canberra, where he gained a Ph.D. in 1992. His studies have taken him on extended field work in remote areas of Papua New Guinea, and he has published articles based on his anthropological research in this region and elsewhere. He has lectured in Polish at the Australian National University, and in anthropology at the ANU and Sydney and Macquarie Universities. He is currently a Lecturer in Anthropology at Macquarie University in Sydney.

He is married with one son and lives in Sydney.

Kevin Windle was born in London in 1947 and educated at Kent College, Canterbury, and Liverpool University, where he took a degree in Russian. He later obtained an M.A. from McMaster University and a Ph.D. from McGill University in Canada. He has lectured in Russian (language and literature) at the University of Queensland in Brisbane and is now a Reader in the School of Language Studies at the Australian National University in Canberra. He has also worked for the BBC Monitoring Service.

He has published numerous translations of works of Russian, Ukrainian and Polish literature, and a number of articles on Russian literature and matters of literary translation. His major publications include *The Routledge Macedonian–English Dictionary* (1998) and the first English translation of Sergei Aksakov's *Notes of a Provincial Wildfowler* (Northwestern University Press, 1998).

He is married with two children and lives in Canberra.

Other titles in the the Routledge Harwood Polish and East European Theatre Archive series:

Volume 10
The Conspiracy of Feelings
Yurii Olesha
and
The Little Theatre of the Green Goose
Konstanty Ildefons Gałczyński
Edited by Daniel Gerould

Volume 11
A Dream
Felicja Kruszewska
and
An Excursion to the Museum
Tadeusz Różewicz
Edited by Jadwiga Kosicka

Volume 12
Mr Price, Or Tropical Madness and Metaphysics of a Two-headed Calf
Stanisław Ignacy Witkiewicz
Edited by Daniel Gerould

This book is part of a series. The publisher will accept continuation orders which may be cancelled at any time and which provide for automatic billing and shipping of each title in the series upon publication. Please write for details.